An Introductory Bibliography
for the Study of Scripture

Woodstock Papers

Occasional Essays for Theology

PREPARED BY
Professors of the Faculty of Theology
Woodstock College, Woodstock, Maryland

EDITED BY
JOHN COURTNEY MURRAY, S.J.
WALTER J. BURGHARDT, S.J.

No. 5

THE NEWMAN PRESS
WESTMINSTER, MARYLAND
1961

An Introductory Bibliography for the Study of Scripture

by GEORGE S. GLANZMAN, S.J.
Professor of the Old Testament

AND

JOSEPH A. FITZMYER, S.J.
Professor of the New Testament
Woodstock College

THE NEWMAN PRESS
WESTMINSTER, MARYLAND
1961

Imprimi Potest: JOHN M. DALEY, S.J.
Praep. Prov. Marylandiae

Nihil Obstat: EDWARD A. CERNY, S.S., D.D.
Censor Librorum

Imprimatur: ✠ FRANCIS P. KEOUGH, D.D.
Archiep. Baltimorensis

November 14, 1960

* Contents *

⋆ Preface ⋆

THE AIM of the compilers of this annotated bibliography is to present a list of titles of reasonable
length with which the student who is beginning theology
or the study of Scripture in a serious way might do well
to familiarize himself. It is not hoped that such a student
would read through all these books, but that he would
acquire some acquaintance with them. In the various
disciplines which make up the complex of Scripture
studies there are many books to which the beginner
might turn. But often he is at a loss in trying to decide
where to begin or to find out which are the standard,
reputable authors in the discipline in which he is inter-
ested. It is the hope of the compilers that this bibliography will guide such a beginner to *basic* titles, which
will enable him to judge others accordingly, and also to
the more important *secondary* works.

This annotated list originated in a need felt by Fr.
Glanzman for supplying a bibliographical guide to his
students in the class of OT. It was found to be so useful
even by others who saw it that publication of it was
urged. It has been completely rewritten and expanded
to include NT counterparts.

A selective bibliography such as this is always open
to the criticism that such or such a title should have been
included. The compilers are all too aware of this diffi-

culty; part of the problem always is where to draw the line. They believe, however, that their efforts will be rewarded, if the "beginner" were to take two weeks out of his life, bury himself in a good library, and browse through the books listed here. Any professor would be happy to find such a "beginner" in his class.

The titles have been ordered under convenient headings: *Periodicals, Series, Introductions,* etc. Under each heading there are often titles which are common to both the OT and the NT; they are followed by what is specifically related to each Testament. In many instances references have been added to reviews of the book in question, as a convenient guide to some estimates of its value. Commonly used abbreviations have also been inserted in the margin to familiarize the reader with them. The asterisk indicates a Catholic author or editor; in the latter case it does not mean that others have not contributed to works so edited; conversely, its absence does not mean the absence of Catholic contributions.

★ List of Abbreviations ★

AAOS

Annual of the American Schools of Oriental Research (§36)

AG

Arndt, W. F., and Gingrich, F. W., *A Greek-English Lexicon of the New Testament and Other Early Christian Literature* (§130)

AJA

American Journal of Archaeology

AJSL

American Journal of Semitic Languages and Literatures (§35)

ANEP

Pritchard, J. B., *The Ancient Near East in Pictures Relating to the Old Testament* (§327)

ANET

Pritchard, J. B. (ed.), *Ancient Near Eastern Texts Relating to the Old Testament* (§328)

AOB, AOT

Gressmann, H., *Altorientalische Texte und Bilder zum Alten Testament* (§323)

ArOr

Archiv Orientální

ATD

Das Alte Testament Deutsch (§191)

ATR

Anglican Theological Review

BA

Biblical Archaeologist (§3)

BASOR

Bulletin of the American Schools of Oriental Research (§38)

BB

Bonnerbibel (§198)

BDB

Brown, F., Driver, S. R., and Briggs, C. A., *A Hebrew and English Lexicon of the Old Testament* (§124)

BenMon

Benediktinische Monatschrift

Bib

Biblica (§2)

BJ

Bible de Jérusalem (§189)

BK

Biblischer Kommentar: Altes Testament (§193)

BNTC

Black's New Testament Commentaries (§200)

BO

Bibliotheca orientalis (§37)

BS

Bibliotheca sacra

BTW

Bauer, J. B. (ed.), *Bibeltheologisches Wörterbuch* (§211)

BVC

Bible et vie chrétienne (§1)

BZ

Biblische Zeitschrift (§4)

CaB

Cambridge Bible for Schools and Colleges (§194)

CBQ

Catholic Biblical Quarterly (§5)

CCD

Confraternity of Christian Doctrine: The Holy Bible (§119)

CCHS

Orchard, B., *Catholic Commentary on Holy Scripture* (§185)

CGTC

Cambridge Greek Testament Commentary (§200)

CHR

Catholic Historical Review

CIR

Clergy Review

CNT

Commentaire du Nouveau Testament (§202)

CP

Classical Philology

CQR

Church Quarterly Review

CRAIBL

Comptes rendus de l'Académie des Inscriptions et Belles-Lettres (§40)

DBS

Cazelles, H. (ed.), *Dictionnaire de la Bible, Supplément* (§212)

EB

Etudes bibliques (§186)

EstBib

Estudios bíblicos (§6)

ETL

Ephemerides theologicae Lovanienses (§17)

ExpTim

Expository Times (§18)

GB

Gesenius, W., and Buhl, F., *Hebräisches und aramäisches Handwörterbuch über das Alte Testament* (§125)

HAT

Handbuch zum Alten Testament (§197)

HDB

Hastings, J. (ed.), *A Dictionary of the Bible* (§217)

HKAT

Göttinger Handkommentar zum Alten Testament (§196)

HJ

Hibbert Journal

HNT

Handbuch zum Neuen Testament (§203)

HS

Die Heilige Schrift des Alten Testaments (= *BB*) (§198)

HThK

Herders Theologischer Kommentar zum Neuen Testament (§204)

IB

Interpreter's Bible (§188)

ICC

International Critical Commentary (§187)

IEJ

Israel Exploration Journal (§41)

IER

Irish Ecclesiastical Record

JAOS

Journal of the American Oriental Society (§43)

JBL

Journal of Biblical Literature (§7)

JBR

Journal of Bible and Religion

JCS

> *Journal of Cuneiform Studies*

JNES

> *Journal of Near Eastern Studies* (§44)

JPOS

> *Journal of the Palestine Oriental Society* (§45)

JQR

> *Jewish Quarterly Review* (§42)

JR

> *Journal of Religion*

JSS

> *Journal of Semitic Studies* (§46)

JTS

> *Journal of Theological Studies* (§20)

KB

> Koehler, L., and Baumgartner, W., *Lexicon in Veteris Testamenti libros* (§126)

KD

> *Kerygma und Dogma* (§21)

LS

> Liddell, H. G., and Scott, R., *A Greek-English Lexicon* (§132)

LXX

> Septuagint

Meyer

> Meyerkommentar (= *Kritisch-exegetischer Kommentar über das Neue Testament*) (§205)

MM

Moulton, J. H., and Milligan, G., *The Vocabulary of the Greek Testament* (§133)

MT

Massoretic Text

MUSJ

Mélanges de l'Université Saint-Joseph (§22)

NovT

Novum Testamentum (§9)

NRT

Nouvelle revue théologique

NT

New Testament

NTA

New Testament Abstracts (§337)

NTD

Das Neue Testament Deutsch (§206)

NTS

New Testament Studies (§8)

OLZ

Orientalistische Literaturzeitung (§48)

Or

Orientalia (§47)

OrChr

Oriens christianus

OT

Old Testament

PEFQS

> *Palestine Exploration Fund, Quarterly Statement* (§50)

PEQ

> *Palestine Exploration Quarterly* (§51)

PJ

> *Palästinajahrbuch* (§49)

PW

> *Paulys Real-Encyclopädie der classischen Altertumswissenschaft* (= RE) (§221)

QDAP

> *Quarterly of the Department of Antiquities of Palestine* (§52)

RB

> *Revue biblique* (§10)

RE

> = *PW* (§221)

RevScRel

> *Revue des sciences religieuses* (§26)

RGG

> *Religion in Geschichte und Gegenwart* (§215)

RHE

> *Revue d'histoire ecclésiastique*

RHPR

> *Revue d'histoire et de philosophie religieuses*

RHR

> *Revue de l'histoire des religions* (§53)

RivBib

Rivista biblica (§11)

RNT

Regensburger Neues Testament (§207)

RQ

Revue de Qumran (§299)

RSO

Rivista degli studi orientali (§54)

RSPT

Revue des sciences philosophiques et théologiques (§25)

RSR

Recherches de science religieuse (§24)

RSV

Revised Standard Version (§120)

Schol

Scholastik

Sef

Sefarad

SJT

Scottish Journal of Theology (§27)

ST

Studia theologica (§28)

ThHK

Theologischer Handkommentar zum Neuen Testament (§208)

ThRev

Theologische Revue

TLZ

Theologische Literaturzeitung (§30)

TQ

Theologische Quartalschrift

TR

Theologische Rundschau (§31)

TS

Theological Studies (§29)

TWNT

Kittel, G. (ed.), *Theologisches Wörterbuch zum Neuen Testament* (§218)

TZ

Theologische Zeitschrift (§32)

VD

Verbum Domini (§13)

VS

Verbum salutis (§209)

VT

Vetus Testamentum (§14)

WO

Die Welt des Orients (§57)

ZAW

Zeitschrift für die alttestamentliche Wissenschaft (§15)

ZDMG

Zeitschrift der deutschen morgenländischen Gesellschaft (§58)

ZDPV

Zeitschrift des deutschen Palästinavereins (§59)

ZKT

Zeitschrift für katholische Theologie (§33)

ZNW

Zeitschrift für die neutestamentliche Wissenschaft und die Kunde des Urchristentums (§16)

ZThK

Zeitschrift für Theologie und Kirche (§34)

An Introductory Bibliography

for the Study of Scripture

QUOD VIDIMUS TESTAMUR

* I. Periodicals *

A. Biblical

BVC   1. *Bible et vie chrétienne* (Paris, 1953—). Published six times a year by the Abbey of Maredsous. Articles on both Testaments; reviews. The journal is popular and is devoted chiefly to the practical side of biblical studies: preaching, liturgy, etc. Language: French.

Bib   2. *Biblica* (Rome, 1920—). Published quarterly by the Jesuits of the Pontificio Istituto Biblico. Articles on both Testaments; shorter notes; news of the scholarly world; archaeological news; reviews. The "Elenchus bibliographicus," which has been greatly expanded and improved since 1949 by Fr. P. Nober, is an indispensable tool. Though the contributions vary in quality, during the last few years this has become a very important journal. Languages: English, French, German, Italian, Latin, Spanish.

BA   3. *The Biblical Archaeologist* (New Haven, 1938—). Published quarterly by the American Schools of Oriental Research. Articles pertinent for both Testaments; occasionally reviews. An excellent little bulletin, less technical than BASOR; it will keep the reader abreast of current archaeological work and interpretation. Language: English.

BZ   4. *Biblische Zeitschrift* (Paderborn, 1903—). Published semiannually under the editorship of V.

Hamp and R. Schnackenburg. The old journal died in 1939 (Vol. 24); the revived journal begins a new series with new numbering, scil., Vol. 1 (1957). Articles on both Testaments; shorter contributions; biblical news; reviews. In its new form this is an important journal. Language: German.

CBQ 5. *The Catholic Biblical Quarterly* (Washington, D.C., 1939—). Published quarterly by the Catholic Biblical Association of America. Articles on both Testaments; shorter notes ("Miscellanea biblica"); scholarly news; archaeological reports; reviews. In recent years the quality of the journal has greatly improved, though there is still a good deal of unevenness. Language: English.

EstBib 6. *Estudios bíblicos* (Madrid, 1929—). Published quarterly by the Association to Foster Biblical Studies in Spain (AFEBE). A new series with new numbering was begun in July–Sept., 1941; Vol. 1 represents 1941–42. Articles on both Testaments; shorter notes; reviews. This is the best of the biblical journals for Spanish readers. Language: Spanish.

JBL 7. *Journal of Biblical Literature* (Philadelphia, 1881—). Published quarterly by the Society of Biblical Literature and Exegesis. Articles on both Testaments; reviews. The contents vary considerably in quality, and almost every shade of biblical position is represented; but this is an important biblical periodical. Eleven supplementary monographs have been published. Language: English, occasionally a French or German contribution.

[4]

NTS 8. *New Testament Studies* (Cambridge, Eng., 1954—). Published quarterly by Studiorum Novi Testamenti Societas, whose *Bulletin* it replaced (only three issues of the latter appeared: 1950, 1951, 1952). Articles on the NT and related fields (Dead Sea Scrolls, Gnosticism, etc.); short studies; reviews. Since NTS is the organ of *the* international NT society, its contributors are among the best in the field, representing all faiths. Languages: English, French, German.

NovT 9. *Novum Testamentum* (Leiden, 1956—). Published by E. J. Brill, intended to be an international quarterly for NT and related studies based on international co-operation. Its sporadic appearance, however, since 1956 is due partly to the boycott of NT scholars, who saw no need for another international periodical when NTS already existed. Consequently, the contributions have so far been of very uneven quality, sometimes rather poor. Articles; book reviews. Languages: English, French, German. (Intended as the NT counterpart of *Vetus Testamentum;* see §14.)

RB 10. **Revue biblique* (Paris, 1892—). Published quarterly by the French Dominicans of L'Ecole Pratique d'Etudes Bibliques in Jerusalem. After Vol. 12 (1903) a new series with new numeration was begun; this ran to Vol. 16 (1919). In 1920 a fresh start was made; the previous collections of twelve and sixteen volumes were counted as one series and continued by Vol. 29 (1920). During the years 1941–45 the journal appeared as *Vivre et penser* and ran through three series; these now correspond to RB 50–52. In 1946, RB was revived with Vol. 53. Articles on both Testaments; chronicles of archaeological work; one or two long reviews. Special attention should be given to the "Bulletin," a large collection of briefer reviews of works on both Testaments and allied fields. This is by far the most important biblical periodical embracing both Testaments. Language: French.

RivBib 11. *Rivista biblica* (Florence, 1953—). Published quarterly by the Italian Biblical Association. Articles on both Testaments; reviews. Language: Italian.

12. *Scripture* (London–Edinburgh, 1946—). Published quarterly by the Catholic Biblical Association (in England). Articles on both Testaments; reviews. Though a semipopular journal, it contains some worth-while contributions. Language: English.

VD 13. *Verbum Domini* (Rome, 1921—). Published six times a year by the Pontificio Istituto Biblico. Publication was interrupted in 1945–46, but revived in 1947. Articles on both Testaments; reviews. The rather extended survey of periodicals and collections ("Spectator ephemeridum et collectaneorum") is valuable. Though the journal is intended to be more popular than scientific, it contains many useful contributions. Language: Latin.

VT 14. *Vetus Testamentum* (Leiden, 1951—). Published quarterly by the International Organization of Old Testament Scholars. Articles on OT and early Judaism; short notes; reviews. The contributions vary greatly in quality. Six supplementary volumes have been published. Languages: English, French, German.

AW 15. *Zeitschrift für die alttestamentliche Wissenschaft* (Berlin, 1881—). Normally published semiannually by an international group of scholars; the editors have been O. Eissfeldt and J. Hempel, but a new editor, G. Fohrer, has recently been named. The journal was founded by B. Stade. In 1924 Gressmann and Hempel became the editors; they started a new series, though the numbering of the volumes was not changed. For the years 1942–50 there were only four volumes (59–62); with Vol. 63 (1951) regular publication resumed. Articles on OT (including deuterocanonical books) and early Judaism; shorter contributions; some reviews of varying length. There is a very valuable section devoted to abstracts of important publications in journals and collections. This is the most important journal devoted to the OT field; for the editors' own view of what the journal should be, cf. the inside back cover of Vol. 71 (1959). Languages: English, German, occasionally French.

NW 16. *Zeitschrift für die neutestamentliche Wissenschaft und die Kunde des Urchristentums* (Berlin, 1900—). Published quarterly by A. Töpelmann under the editorship of top-ranking German Protestant scholars, at first E. Preuschen, later H. Lietzmann, at present W. Bauer and J. Jeremias. Articles on the NT and related fields; a useful "Zeitschriften-Bibliographie." The best of German Protestant NT contributions are found in this magazine; Catholic scholars also contribute to it occasionally. Fifty volumes have appeared to date. The two wars interrupted its publication somewhat;

[7]

Vols. 18–19 covered the years 1917–20; after Vol. 41 (1942) ZNW did not appear for six years; Vol. 42 was issued in 1949, and Vol. 43 covered 1950–51, Vol. 44 1952–53. Since 1954 it has appeared regularly in double issues twice a year. Language: usually German, occasionally English.

Much material pertinent to biblical studies will be found in theological journals and in periodicals relating to Palestine and the Near East. The following is a selection listing the most important and most useful.

B. Theological

ETL 17. *Ephemerides theologicae Lovanienses* (Louvain, 1924—).

ExpTim 18. *The Expository Times* (Edinburgh, 1889—).

19. *Interpretation: A Journal of Bible and Theology* (Richmond, Va., 1947—). Continues *Union Seminary Review.*

JTS 20. *The Journal of Theological Studies* (Oxford, 1899—).

KD 21. *Kerygma und Dogma* (Göttingen, 1955—).

MUSJ 22. *Mélanges de l'Université Saint-Joseph* (Beirut, 1906—).

23. *Muséon* (Louvain, 1881—).

RSR 24. *Recherches de science religieuse* (Paris, 1910—).

RSPT 25. *Revue des sciences philosophiques et théologiques* (Paris, 1907—).

el 26. *Revue des sciences religieuses* (Strasbourg, 1921—).

JT 27. *Scottish Journal of Theology* (Edinburgh, 1948—).

ST 28. *Studia theologica* (Lund, 1948—).

TS 29. **Theological Studies* (Woodstock, Md., 1940—).

LZ 30. *Theologische Literaturzeitung* (Leipzig, 1876—).

TR 31. *Theologische Rundschau* (Tübingen, 1897—).

TZ 32. *Theologische Zeitschrift* (Basel, 1945—).

KT 33. **Zeitschrift für katholische Theologie* (Innsbruck–Vienna, 1877—).

hK 34. *Zeitschrift für Theologie und Kirche* (Tübingen, 1891—).

C. Near East and General

JSL 35. *American Journal of Semitic Languages and Literatures* (Chicago, 1895–1941).

OS 36. *Annual of the American Schools of Oriental Research* (New Haven, 1919/20—).

BO 37. *Bibliotheca orientalis* (Leiden, 1943—).

OR 38. *Bulletin of the American Schools of Oriental Research* (New Haven, 1919—).

39. **Cahiers Sioniens* (Paris, 1947—).

IBL 40. *Comptes rendus de l'Académie des Inscriptions et Belles-Lettres* (Paris, 1857—).

IEJ 41. *Israel Exploration Journal* (Jerusalem, 1950/51—).

JQR   42.   *Jewish Quarterly Review* (Philadelphia, 1888—).

JAOS   43.   *Journal of the American Oriental Society* (New Haven, 1843—).

JNES   44.   *Journal of Near Eastern Studies* (Chicago, 1942—). Continues AJSL.

JPOS   45.   *Journal of the Palestine Oriental Society* (Jerusalem, 1921–37).

JSS   46.   *Journal of Semitic Studies* (Manchester, 1956—).

Or   47.   *Orientalia (Rome, 1920—).

OLZ   48.   *Orientalistische Literaturzeitung* (Leipzig–Berlin, 1898—).

PJ   49.   *Palästinajahrbuch* (Berlin, 1905–41).

PEFQS   50.   *Palestine Exploration Fund, Quarterly Statement* (London, 1869–1936).

PEQ   51.   *Palestine Exploration Quarterly* (London, 1937—). Continues PEFQS.

QDAP   52.   *Quarterly of the Department of Antiquities of Palestine* (Jerusalem, 1932–50).

RHR   53.   *Revue de l'histoire des religions* (Paris, 1880—).

RSO   54.   *Rivista degli studi orientali* (Rome, 1907—).

    55.   *Semitica* (Paris, 1948—).

    56.   *Syria* (Paris, 1920—).

WO   57.   *Die Welt des Orients* (Stuttgart, 1947—).

ZDMG   58.   *Zeitschrift der deutschen morgenländischen Gesellschaft* (Wiesbaden, 1847—).

ZDPV   59.   *Zeitschrift des deutschen Palästinavereins* (Bonn, 1878—).

⋆ II. Series ⋆

The following series and collections are devoted either wholly or in large part to biblical studies; they contain important monographs and papers.

60. *Abhandlungen zur Theologie des Alten und Neuen Testaments* (Zurich, 1942—).

61. *Acta seminarii neotestamentici* (Uppsala, 1935—).

62 *Alttestamentliche Abhandlungen* (Münster i. W., 1909–40).

63. *Analecta biblica* (Rome, 1952—).

64. *Analecta Lovaniensia biblica et orientalia* (Louvain, 1947—). Continues *Bulletin d'histoire et d'exégèse de l'Ancien Testament*.

65. *Beihefte zur Zeitschrift für die alttestamentliche Wissenschaft* (Berlin, 1896—).

66. *Beihefte zur Zeitschrift für die neutestamentliche Wissenschaft* (Berlin, 1923—).

67. *Beiträge zur historischen Theologie* (Tübingen, 1929—).

68. *Beiträge zur Wissenschaft vom Alten (und Neuen) Testament* (Leipzig-Stuttgart, 1908—). Nothing has appeared since World War II.

69. *Bible Key Words from Gerhard Kittel's Theo-*

logisches Wörterbuch zum Neuen Testament (London, 1949—).

70. *Bonner biblische Beiträge* (Bonn, 1950—).

71. *Bulletin d'histoire et d'exégèse de l'Ancien Testament* (Louvain, 1934-47).

72. *Cahiers théologiques* (Neuchâtel, 1943—).

73. *Coniectanea neotestamentica* (Uppsala, 1936—).

74. *Forschungen zur Religion und Literatur des Alten und Neuen Testaments* (Göttingen, 1903—).

75. *Hebrew Union College Annual* (Cincinnati, 1924—).

76. *Neutestamentliche Abhandlungen* (Münster i. W., 1908—).

77. *Oudtestamentische Studiën* (Leiden, 1942—).

78. *Recherches bibliques* (Louvain, 1954—).

79. *Studies in Biblical Theology* (London, 1950—).

80. *Studii biblici Franciscani liber annuus* (Jerusalem, 1950—).

81. *Svensk exegetisk årsbok* (Uppsala, 1936—).

82. *Symbolae biblicae Upsalienses* (Uppsala, 1943—). Supplements to *Svensk exegetisk årsbok*.

83. *Uppsala Universitets årsskrift* (Uppsala, 1861—).

* III. Introductions to the Biblical Text and Ancient Versions *

A. OT

84. Ginsburg, C., *Introduction to the Massoretico-Critical Edition of the Hebrew Bible* (London: Trinitarian Bible Society, 1897). The value of this massive work is greatly diminished by many false statements and misleading information.

    Cf. B. J. Roberts, *The Old Testament Text and Versions,* pp. 79–80.

85. Rahlfs, A., *Verzeichnis der griechischen Handschriften des Alten Testaments* (Berlin: Weidmann, 1914). A list of approximately two thousand MSS and fragments of the Greek OT; gives their date, size, present location, contents, etc. A very valuable tool for the study of the LXX.

86. Roberts, B. J., *The Old Testament Text and Versions* (Cardiff: University of Wales Press, 1951). In spite of shortcomings, a very valuable handbook on the subject. The student will profit by the careful descriptions and analyses of older works, and the clear statement of problems; the bibliography is very rich.

    Cf. Bib 32 (1951) 441–47; TLZ 76 (1951) 535–39; VT 1 (1951) 238–40; *Eleven Years of Bible Bibliography,* p. 326; RB 59 (1952) 439–40.

87. Swete, H. B., *An Introduction to the Old Testament in Greek* (2nd ed. rev. by R. R. Ottley; Cambridge: University Press, 1914). Still the most comprehensive and useful introduction to the text of the LXX.

88. Würthwein, E., *The Text of the Old Testament: An Introduction to Kittel-Kahle's Biblia Hebraica* (tr. by P. Ackroyd; Oxford: Blackwell, 1957). The German original appeared in 1952. As an introduction and guide to the third and subsequent editions of Kittel, the book has value, but it also serves to point up the deficiencies of Kittel-Kahle.
     Cf. TLZ 78 (1953) 332 f.; ZAW 65 (1953) 108; *Eleven Years of Bible Bibliography*, p. 483; JSS 4 (1959) 149–51.

B. NT

89. Colwell, E. C., *What Is the Best New Testament?* (Chicago: University of Chicago Press, 1952). A popular, nontechnical sketch of the history of the NT text since Erasmus. It contains a description of the Anglo-American project to construct a thorough *apparatus criticus* for every NT verse.
     Cf. JBL 71 (1952) 188; RB 60 (1953) 439–40.

90. Gregory, C. R., *Textkritik des Neuen Testaments* (Leipzig: Hinrichs, 1900–1909). It offers a very complete general account of the Greek MSS and lectionaries used for NT textual criticism. It goes beyond the Prolegomena of Tischendorf's *editio maior*. Still useful.
     Cf. JTS 3 (1901–2) 295–96.

[14]

91. Kenyon, F. G., *Handbook to the Textual Criticism of the New Testament* (2nd ed.; London: Macmillan, 1926). A basic text by a famous scholar; the "best of its kind by an Englishman" (K. Lake).
Cf. JTS 3 (1901–2) 296–97.

92. Kraft, B., *Die Zeichen für die wichtigeren Handschriften des griechischen Neuen Testaments* (3rd ed.; Freiburg: Herder, 1955). First edition, 1926; second, 1934. An indispensable tool for the resolution of the conflict in methods of reference to the NT MSS. Intended chiefly as an aid to von Soden's edition, it has very useful cross references to the editions of Tischendorf, Wettstein, and Gregory.
Cf. JTS n.s. 6 (1955) 347; CBQ 17 (1955) 535; TLZ 80 (1955) 655.

93. *Lagrange, M.-J., *Introduction à l'étude du Nouveau Testament. Deuxième partie (Critique textuelle) 2: La critique rationnelle* (Etudes bibliques; Paris: Gabalda, 1935). A thorough discussion of the many problems of NT textual criticism, containing a general survey of the history and study of the NT text. Detailed bibliography can be found here. "The most intelligible general statement on the subject since Westcott and Hort's 'Introduction'" (S. Lake).
Cf. Bib 20 (1939) 458–60; RSR 17 (1937) 42–51; RHPR 18 (1938) 187–89; JBL 55 (1936) 95–97.

94. Nestle, E., *Einführung in das griechische Neue Testament* (4th ed. rev. by E. von Dobschütz; Göttingen: Vandenhoeck & Ruprecht, 1923). A basic book for beginners in the study of NT textual

criticism. Three parts contain (1) a history of the text, MSS, versions, and printed editions; (2) materials and methods of textual criticism; (3) twenty-three photographic reproductions of original MSS. Earlier editions (1897, 1899, 1909) still contain many useful points that were crowded out of subsequent revisions; von Dobschütz's fourth edition changed the arrangement somewhat and recast the whole work. An English translation of the second edition was made by W. Edie, entitled *Introduction to the Textual Criticism of the Greek New Testament* (New York: G. P. Putnam, 1901). Cf. HTR 17 (1924) 91–94; ZNW 22 (1923) 312–13.

95. Soden, H. von, *Die Schriften des Neuen Testaments in ihrer ältesten erreichbaren Textgestalt hergestellt auf Grund ihrer Textgeschichte* (Göttingen: Vandenhoeck & Ruprecht, Vol. 1 [in 3 parts; 2nd ed.] 1911; Vol. 2, 1913). Divided the NT MS families into three recensions: K (*Koine* = Antiochene or Syrian), H (*Hesychian* = Egyptian or Alexandrian), I (*Jerusalem* or Palestinian). The text is eclectic; the *apparatus criticus* is abundant, and much information about the NT text is to be found only here. Though it is in many ways still indispensable, it must be used with care, since many scholars do not agree with the principles on which von Soden's text is based.
Cf. JTS 15 (1914) 307–26; CQR 79 (1914–15) 57–68; Bib 4 (1923) 180–89; ZNW 8 (1907) 34–47.

96. Kenyon, F., *Our Bible and the Ancient Manuscripts* (5th ed. rev. by A. W. Adams; London:

Eyre and Spottiswoode, 1958). An excellent, readable account of the texts of the OT and NT and of
the problems involved in the transmission of texts.
First published in 1895, it was substantially enlarged in 1939 and now appears in its fifth edition.
Cf. JR 21 (1941) 330; ExpTim 69 (1957–58) 295–96.

Attention is called to the articles on text and versions in
the various biblical dictionaries.

★ IV. Biblical Texts and Ancient Versions ★

A. MT

97. Ginsburg, C. D., *The Old Testament Diligently Revised according to the Massorah and the Early Editions with the Various Readings from the Manuscripts and the Ancient Versions* (4 vols.; London: British and Foreign Bible Society, 1926). The text was first published in 1894 for the Trinitarian Bible Society; the 1926 edition was based on the same text and finished, after Ginsburg's death, by others. The text used was ben Ḥayim, with collations of about seventy-three MSS mostly from the British Museum and consultation of older and younger printed editions. "The edition is censured mainly because of uncritical use of the Massorah, and eclectic methods of dealing with manuscripts. . . . On the whole the work remains but another and poorer copy of the ben Chayim text." Cf. B. J. Roberts, *The Old Testament Text and Versions,* pp. 89–90.

98. Kittel, R. (ed.), *Biblia Hebraica* (9th ed.; Stuttgart: Württembergische Bibelanstalt, 1954). For his first two editions, Kittel employed a text of ben Ḥayim; beginning with the third edition in 1937,

Kahle introduced the Leningrad text of ben Asher, which has been reprinted in subsequent editions. After the discovery of the Qumrân scrolls, a woefully inadequate attempt was made to include in the *apparatus criticus* the variants from 1QIs^a and 1QpHab. Though Kittel's remains the handiest and most popular edition of the Hebrew Bible, its shortcomings are notorious; the suggested emendations and supposed Hebrew equivalents of LXX readings can be almost completely disregarded.

99. Snaith, N. H. (ed.), *Old Testament in Hebrew* (London: British and Foreign Bible Society, 1958). A handy edition of the Hebrew Bible based on Spanish MSS in the British Museum; according to the editor, these MSS preserve the authentic ben Asher text. The text itself is little different from that of Kittel's third and following editions, though the paragraph divisions and the final Massorah show divergence.

Cf. *Book List* (1959) p. 15; RB 66 (1959) 607.

B. LXX

100. Brooke, A. E., McLean, N., Thackeray, H. St. J., *The Old Testament in Greek* (Cambridge: University Press, Vol. 1 [The Octateuch] 1906–17; Vol. 2 [The Later Historical Books] 1927–35; Vol. 3, Part 1 [Esther, Judith, Tobit] 1940). This edition does not attempt to restore an original LXX; the text of B, with supplements from other uncial MSS, is printed, and an extensive *apparatus criticus* presents the variants of other uncials, cursives, and some

versions. This is an absolutely indispensable tool for study of the Greek Bible and for OT textual criticism.

101. Rahlfs, A., *Septuaginta* (3rd ed.; 2 vols.; Stuttgart: Württembergische Bibelanstalt, 1949). The work was first published in 1935, and all subsequent "editions" are merely reprints. The text is Rahlfs's own reconstruction of the "Septuagint" based on the uncials A, B, and S; there is a short *apparatus criticus* including these and a few other MSS. The work was intended as a manual edition to serve the needs of clergy and students; as such, it is the most convenient and most popular of all LXX editions. But it labors from obvious defects: an eclectic text and insufficient MS evidence; the user must be cautioned against drawing ready arguments for textual emendation or interpretation on the basis of Rahlfs's text.

Cf. ZAW 60 (1944) 128–29.

102. *Septuaginta: Vetus Testamentum Graecum auctoritate Societatis Göttingensis editum* (Göttingen: Vandenhoeck & Ruprecht, 1931—). This great edition was begun in 1931 under the direction of A. Rahlfs for the Septuaginta-Unternehmen of the Göttingen Academy of Sciences. The aim is not to present any one text, but, after careful and extensive study of families or groups of texts, to reconstruct a text which will be the oldest and closest to the original LXX (cf. B. Roberts, *The Old Testament Text and Versions,* pp. 164–67). The work is to be completed in sixteen volumes; so far, the

following have appeared: 9/1 (*Maccabaeorum Liber I;* ed. W. Kappler, 1936); 9/2 (*Maccabaeorum Liber II;* ed. R. Hanhart, 1959); 10 (*Psalmi cum Odis;* ed. A. Rahlfs, 1931); 13 (*Duodecim prophetae;* ed. J. Ziegler, 1943); 14 (*Isaias;* ed. J. Ziegler, 1939); 15 (*Jeremias–Baruch–Threni–Epistula Jeremiae;* ed. J. Ziegler, 1957); 16/1 (*Ezechiel;* ed. J. Ziegler, 1952); 16/1 (*Susanna–Daniel–Bel et Draco;* ed. J. Ziegler, 1954).

103. Swete, H. B., *The Old Testament in Greek* (Cambridge: University Press, Vol. 1 [Genesis–4 Kings, 4th ed.] 1909; Vol. 2 [1 Chronicles–Tobit, 3rd ed.] 1905; Vol. 3 [Hosea–4 Maccabees, 3rd ed.] 1907). This manual edition of the LXX was first published between 1887 and 1894. The text of B is printed, and its lacunae are filled in from A and S; the *apparatus criticus* supplies readings from these latter and from a few other early uncials. In contrast to the text of Rahlfs, this edition has the advantage of giving a single text; but M. L. Margolis, during his study of Joshua, found numerous inaccuracies in Swete's edition, and J. Ziegler, after his study of Amos, concluded that Swete's edition is unsatisfactory for scientific textual criticism.
     Cf. AJSL 28 (1911–12) 3; ZAW 60 (1944) 128.

C. NT

104. *Bover, I. M., *Novi Testamenti Biblia Graeca et Latina* (3rd ed.; Madrid: Consejo Superior de Investigaciones Científicas, 1953). A resultant text

based on the agreements of the big critical editions; where these vary, the reading adopted is that supported by the best testimony of the most ancient codices, versions, and ecclesiastical writers. Critical editions used: Tischendorf, Westcott-Hort, Weiss, von Soden, Vogels, Lagrange. In general, his text recedes from the Alexandrian type and approaches that of the Western and Caesarean; thus it agrees more with von Soden, Vogels, and Merk than with Tischendorf, Westcott-Hort, and Weiss.

Cf. JBL 66 (1947) 415–22; Sef 4 (1944) 199–204; EstBibl 3 (1944) 459–62.

105. Legg, S. C. E., *Nouum Testamentum Graece secundum textum Westcotto-Hortianum: Euangelium secundum Marcum cum apparatu critico nouo plenissimo, lectionibus codicum nuper repertorum additis, editionibus uersionum antiquarum et Patrum ecclesiasticorum denuo inuestigatis* (Oxford: Clarendon Press, 1935). . . . *Euangelium secundum Matthaeum* . . .(*ibid.*, 1940). An ambitious project, rather severely criticized by scholars.

Cf. RB 44 (1935) 623–24; ATR 17 (1935) 172–73; *Gnomon* 13 (1937) 53; JTS 43 (1942) 30–34; *ibid.* 83–92.

106. *Merk, A., *Novum Testamentum Graece et Latine* (8th ed.; Rome: Pontificio Istituto Biblico, 1959). First published in 1933, its Greek text was based on von Soden's text I. But from the fourth and fifth editions on, this text was abandoned and present editions offer an eclectic text based on the evidence of the best MSS, ancient versions, readings of ecclesiastical writers, and critical studies. "Any

scholar who seeks to gain as full a picture of the evidence [of NT MSS readings] as possible and neglects Merk, does so at his own peril" (Kilpatrick).

Cf. JTS 50 (1949) 142-52; RB 53 (1946) 595-97 (reviews of fifth edition).

107. Nestle, E., *Novum Testamentum Graece et Latine* (23rd ed.; Stuttgart: Württembergische Bibelanstalt, 1957). This most widely used pocket edition of the Greek and Latin NT was first published in 1898. The first editor, Eberhard Nestle, aimed at constructing a text not based on his own opinions nor on the Textus Receptus, but on the critical editions of Tischendorf and Westcott-Hort. When they agreed, he reproduced their agreement; when they differed, he consulted Weymouth's *Resultant Greek Testament* and Weiss's *Das Neue Testament* for support. Editions from 1927 on, however, continued by the son Erwin, contain evidence from MS witnesses as well; it has a rich but compact *apparatus criticus*. K. Aland is the editor of the twenty-third edition of this indispensable average, eclectic text of the NT.

Cf. JTS 50 (1949) 10-19 (review of seventeenth edition, 1941); especially NTS 6 (1960) 179-84.

108. Souter, A., *Novum Testamentum Graece: Textui a retractoribus anglis adhibito brevem adnotationem criticam subiecit* (2nd ed.; Oxford: Clarendon Press, 1947). It offers the Greek text underlying the Revised Version of 1881, which "represented a compromise between a bad text and a

good one, between the Textus Receptus and West-cott-Hort" (Kilpatrick).

Cf. JTS 18 (1917) 250–51; JTS n.s. 1 (1950) 19–23.

109. Tischendorf, C., *Novum Testamentum Graece* (8th ed.; 2 vols.; Leipzig: Giesecke und Devrient, 1869, 1872). Vol. 3, *Prolegomena,* was written by C. R. Gregory (3 parts; Leipzig: J. C. Hinrichs, 1884, 1890, 1894). It contains a thorough *apparatus criticus,* which even today is indispensable for many problems.

Cf. CQR 39 (1894–95) 137–59.

110. *Vogels, H. J., *Novum Testamentum Graece et Latine* (2 vols.; 3rd ed.; Freiburg: Herder, 1949–50). This text is not based on the consensus of modern critical editions, but on a number of original authorities (i.e., MSS) themselves. Its short *apparatus criticus* supplies variants from the important majuscules and the chief minuscules, readings of the Fathers, the Old Latin and Syriac versions. Quite useful. First edition, 1922; first edition of Greek text alone, 1920. The text varies little from von Soden.

Cf. Bib 2 (1921) 78–87; 5 (1924) 86–88; JTS 22 (1921) 174–75; TS 11 (1950) 141–42.

111. Westcott, B. F., and Hort, F. J. A., *The New Testament in the Original Greek* (2 vols.; rev. ed.; Cambridge–London: Macmillan, 1890–96). The first edition appeared in 1881 and a larger edition in 1885. It has justly been recognized as a landmark in the printed editions of the NT. Though the authors distinguished the various NT MSS into

four textual forms: the Syrian (Antiochene) text which underlay the Textus Receptus, the Western (Codex D, Vetus Latina), the Alexandrian, and the Neutral text (chiefly Vaticanus and Sinaiticus), they based their edition mainly on the last. Even though present-day textual criticism has gone far beyond Westcott-Hort, their edition nevertheless remains one of the best of the major critical texts of the end of the last century.

Cf. CQR 12 (1881) 514–21; 13 (1882) 419–51.

112. Huck, A., *Synopsis of the First Three Gospels* (9th ed. rev. by H. Lietzmann; Eng. ed. by F. L. Cross; Oxford: Blackwell, 1957). "Each of the three Gospels is printed continuously word for word in its proper column and in unaltered order and the corresponding parallel passages are repeated as many times as this principle demands. As a result the form is independent of any particular theory about sources and can be readily used for studies from any angle" (Preface). This is an indispensable tool for the study of the Synoptic Gospels. "No better synopsis for general use" (Bethune-Baker). Parallels from the Agrapha are added in footnotes; the sixth edition had an appendix in which Johannine parallels were given, but this has been abandoned in recent editions. Originally the Greek text was that of Tischendorf-Gebhardt, but this has been modified in subsequent editions.

Cf. JTS 13 (1912) 634–45; 25 (1923–24) 221–22; 37 (1936) 208–10; RB 45 (1936) 296.

113. Larfeld, W., *Griechische Synopse der vier neutes-*

tamentlichen Evangelien (Tübingen: J. C. B. Mohr, 1911). Taking Mark, the oldest Gospel, as the framework of his synopsis, Larfeld inserts non-Marcan material of the other three Gospels into this framework, in what he judges to be its historical order and sequence. The order of pericopes is therefore rather arbitrary, and for this reason his synopsis has never been as successful as Huck's. The Greek text used is that of Nestle with an *apparatus criticus;* words which are common to two or more Gospels are printed in bold-faced type. Useful when a study of John and the Synoptics is being made.

Cf. JTS 13 (1912) 635.

D. Latin

114. **Biblia sacra juxta Latinam Vulgatam versionem ad codicum fidem . . . cura et studio monachorum abbatiae pontificiae s. Hieronymi in Urbe ordinis sancti Benedicti edita* (Rome: Typis Polyglottis Vaticanis, 1926—). So far, eleven volumes, covering most of the OT, have appeared. The edition was launched in 1907 under the direction of Card. Gasquet (cf. "Vulgate, Revision of," *Catholic Encyclopedia* 15, 515–20, for Gasquet's own description of the undertaking). The aim "is to determine as accurately as possible the text of St. Jerome's Latin translation, made in the fourth century." H. Quentin was appointed editor, and he established the principles on which the work proceeds. While the principles of editing have been severely

criticized, and though the resulting text cannot be called the original Vulgate of Jerome, this edition has very great importance for the history of the Vulgate and for the textual criticism of the Hebrew OT; a cursory comparison of this text with the Clementine Vulgate will convince the student that many readings have been erroneously going by the name "Vulgate."

Cf. Bib 11 (1930) 458–64; B. J. Roberts, *The Old Testament Text and Versions,* pp. 260–62.

115. *Biblia sacra Vulgatae editionis . . . editio emenda-tissima* (Turin: Marietti, 1959). The most recent handy edition of the Clementine recension of the Vulgate. Edited with critical apparatus and marginal cross references by the Benedictines of St. Jerome's Abbey in Rome. It includes, in addition to the Gallican Psalter, Jerome's Psalter *juxta Hebraeos* and the new Biblical Institute version of the Psalms.

116. *Hetzenauer, M., *Biblia sacra Vulgatae editionis* (3rd ed.; Ratisbon: Pustet, 1929). The best handy edition of the Sixtine-Clementine Vulgate; a very brief *apparatus criticus* and an appendix (after Angelo Rocca) showing the differences between the Clementine edition and the Hebrew and Greek texts.

117. *Vetus Latina: Die Reste der altlateinischen Bibel nach Petrus Sabatier neu gesammelt und heraus-gegeben von der Erzabtei Beuron* (Freiburg: Herder, 1949—). This monumental work is to be completed in twenty-seven volumes; it will cover both

OT and NT. In 1949, B. Fischer published a first volume (*Verzeichnis der Sigel für Handschriften und Kirchenschriftsteller*), and from 1951 to 1954 a second volume (*Genesis*); of Vol. 26 (Catholic Epistles and Apocalypse), two fascicles appeared in 1956 and 1958. This work will be an indispensable tool for the study of a very important ancient version.

Cf. RB 58–60, 62, 63; *Eleven Years of Bible Bibliography,* pp. 326, 396, 482, 566, 661; *Forschungen und Fortschritte* 29 (1959) 46–57; TS 21 (1960) 62–63.

117a. Wordsworth, J., and White, H. J., *Nouum Testamentum Domini nostri Jesu Christi Latine secundum editionem s. Hieronymi ad codicum manuscriptorum fidem* (3 vols.; Oxford: Clarendon, 1889–1954). This is the great critical edition of the Latin Vulgate text of the NT. The Gospels appeared fairly rapidly between 1889 and 1895, but the rest of the NT was slow in being published (Acts, 1905; Romans, 1911; the rest of Paul, 1941; final part, 1954). The tedious work was slowed up by the consultation of many more MSS after the Gospels were published and then by the death of Wordsworth in 1911 and White in 1934. Prominent English scholars collaborated in various phases of the work, and after 1934 it was under the direction of H. F. D. Sparks. It is an indispensable *instrument de travail,* whose high scientific value and merits have often been pointed out.

Cf. ZNW 46 (1955) 178–96; JTS 43 (1942) 98–99; NRT 76 (1954) 544.

★ V. English Versions ★

It would be both impossible and needless to give a full account of all the English translations of the Bible which have appeared in the last 400 years. We have selected a few for description because we feel that they are important for modernity and critical value. For further details on the history of the English Bible, the student may confer the convenient summaries in H. W. Robinson, *The Bible in Its Ancient and English Versions* (Oxford, 1940) pp. 128–274 (with bibliography); H. Pope, *English Versions of the Bible* (rev. ed.; St. Louis, 1952); F. Kenyon, *Our Bible and the Ancient Manuscripts* (rev. ed.; New York, 1958) pp. 265–331. For a detailed critical review of modern English translations of the OT, cf. E. Arbez, "Modern Translations of the Old Testament: V. English Language Translations," CBQ 17 (1955) 456–85.

118. *The Complete Bible: An American Translation* (rev. ed.; Chicago: University of Chicago Press, 1939). An independent translation, often called the "Chicago Bible." In 1923, E. J. Goodspeed published a translation of the NT into modern English, based on the text of Westcott-Hort; it was entitled *The New Testament: An American Translation.* In 1927, a translation of the OT was issued by a group of scholars under the editorship of J. M.

[31]

Powis Smith; this edition contained nearly one hundred pages of closely printed textual notes to justify the version, but unfortunately these have been omitted in later editions. In 1935, this translation was revised by T. J. Meek with the assistance of L. Waterman. In 1938, Goodspeed issued his *The Apocrypha: An American Translation*. Finally, in 1939, all these works were combined to form a very valuable complete Bible.

Goodspeed's English translation of the Greek text of the Westcott-Hort NT has been justly hailed as an extraordinary accomplishment. "A comparison of the modern versions raises one's esteem of G as nothing else will. He was the first to break out of the chains of 'Bible English,' and he not only broke out, he shattered the chains" (J. L. McKenzie). An edition which contains this translation face to face with the Greek text of Westcott-Hort is *The Student's New Testament: The Greek Text and the American Translation* (Chicago: University of Chicago Press, 1954).

Cf. ExpTim 35 (1923–24) 110–11.

CCD 119. *The Holy Bible: Confraternity of Christian Doctrine* (Paterson, N.J.; St. Anthony Guild Press, Vol. 1 [1953], Vol. 3 [1955]). This is an authorized translation of the OT and NT, sponsored by the Episcopal Committee of the Confraternity of Christian Doctrine and prepared by members of the Catholic Biblical Association of America. It is a new translation from the original languages with use of the ancient versions. The OT will be completed in four volumes, of which Genesis–Ruth

(Vol. 1) and the Wisdom Literature (Vol. 3) have appeared; the translation of the prophets is now in press. The translation of the NT is still in preparation.

Cf. *Eleven Years of Bible Bibliography,* pp. 486, 731; *Scripture* 6 (1954) 186–88; 8 (1956) 123–25; RB 61 (1954) 512–13; 63 (1956) 591–92; Bib 35 (1954) 512–13; 39 (1958) 94–95; TS 17 (1956) 237–40; JBL 74 (1955) 281–83; CBQ 18 (1956) 314–15.

The current CCD New Testament is not a translation of the original Greek text, but of the Vulgate, as its title indicates, *The New Testament of Our Lord and Savior Jesus Christ, Translated from the Latin Vulgate* (Paterson, N.J.: St. Anthony Guild Press, 1941).

Cf. AER 104 (1941) 1–11, 120–28, 220–30.

RSV 120. *The Holy Bible: Revised Standard Version* (New York: Nelson, 1952). *The New Covenant: Commonly Called the New Testament of Our Lord and Savior Jesus Christ. Revised Standard Version. Translated from the Greek, Being the Version Set Forth A.D. 1611, Revised A.D. 1881 and A.D. 1901, Compared with the Most Ancient Authorities and Revised A.D. 1946* (New York: Nelson, 1946). A translation of the OT (according to the Hebrew canon) and NT, prepared under the direction of the Division of Education of the National Council of Churches of Christ in America. It is an authorized revision of the American Standard Version of 1901, which was itself a revision of the King James version (1611). The Greek text used in the NT section differs little from Westcott-Hort. The translation was executed by a number of prominent Protestant OT and NT scholars. As a *revision* of a former translation, it should not be regarded as "a new translation in the language of today."

Cf. for the OT: JQR 43 (1952) 381–84; *Interpretation* 7 (1953) 338–44; ATR 36 (1954) 111–23; CBQ 17 (1955) 88–90; *Eleven Years of Bible Bibliography,* pp. 485–86. For the NT: K. W. Grobel, JBL 66 (1947) 361–84; TS 7 (1946) 321–25; JTS 49 (1948) 118–24.

An Introduction to the Revised Standard Version of the Old Testament (New York: Nelson, 1952). This very useful little brochure, prepared by twelve members of the revision committee of the RSV under the general direction of L. Weigle, intends to furnish the general reader with some idea of the principles which guided the makers of the RSV.

121. *The Apocrypha: Revised Standard Version* (New York: Nelson, 1957). This translation includes the deuterocanonical books, 1–2 Esdras, and the Prayer of Manasseh. The basic Greek text adopted is that of Rahlfs; for 2 Esdras, the basic text is the Vetus Latina in the edition of R. L. Bensly.

Cf. RB 66 (1959) 607; *Theology Today* 14 (1957) 420–26; *Book List* (1958) 19; JBL 78 (1959) 253–55.

122. *The Holy Scriptures according to the Masoretic Text* (Philadelphia: Jewish Publication Society of America, 1917). This translation was issued by an editorial board consisting of representatives of the Jewish Theological Seminary of America, Hebrew Union College of Cincinnati, and Dropsie College of Philadelphia; the editor in chief was M. Margolis. Though the translation was to take into

account existing English versions, ancient versions, and the work of Jewish and non-Jewish scholars, it was to remain a translation for the people; hence, it was stated, one traditional text had to be followed. The basic text chosen was the edition of Baer, with supplement for the lacunae from Ginsburg's edition. The work rests heavily on Jewish tradition from the Talmud and medieval commentators.

123. *Kleist, J. A., and Lilly, J. L., *The New Testament, Rendered from the Original Greek with Explanatory Notes* (Milwaukee: Bruce, 1954). A posthumous publication of a translation of the Greek text into accurate, easily understood American English. The Greek text used is that of Bover (1944). Kleist's translation of the Gospels is far superior to that of Lilly's work on the other parts of the NT. "Best existing translation in English by Catholics . . . ; consistently superior to Knox in the Gospels, superior (but less consistently) to Knox in the other books" (McKenzie).
Cf. CBQ 16 (1954) 491–500; IER 83 (1955) 195–200.

⋆ VI. Lexica ⋆

A. Hebrew and Aramaic

DB 124. Brown, F., Driver, S. R., and Briggs, C. A., *A Hebrew and English Lexicon of the Old Testament* (corrected impression; Oxford: Clarendon Press, 1952). The dictionary includes both Hebrew and Aramaic; words are not arranged in alphabetic order, but according to "stems." Though the etymologies can rarely be trusted, and though many translations must now be rejected, the work is still valuable for the abundance of its references to biblical passages. For the corrected impression, G. R. Driver inserted only those corrections which could be made without resetting the sheets.

GB 125. Gesenius, W., *Hebräisches und aramäisches Handwörterbuch über das Alte Testament* (16th ed. by F. Buhl; Leipzig: Vogel, 1915). All subsequent editions are reprints of the sixteenth. Though largely supplanted by more recent work, this still remains a valuable reference tool.

KB 126. Koehler, L., and Baumgartner, W., *Lexicon in Veteris Testamenti libros* (2nd ed.; Leiden: Brill, 1958). The second edition is a reprint of the 1953 edition, together with a very important supplementary volume of over 225 pages which incorporates a German-Hebrew and German-Aramaic index and a vast number of corrections and additions. Meanings and discussions are given in both German and English; the English translations are at times weak or even ludicrous. The Aramaic section by Baumgartner is by far the better part. If constant reference is made to the supplement, this is an indispensable tool.

Cf. reviews of the various fascicles by P. Humbert in TZ 5–7 (1949–51); 10 (1954); VT 5 (1955); JSS 4 (1959) 147–48.

127. Kuhn, K. G., *Rückläufiges hebräisches Wörterbuch* (Göttingen: Vandenhoeck & Ruprecht, 1958). A useful reverse dictionary which claims to include all the words of the Hebrew Bible, Ben Sira, the Qumrân materials from Cave 1 (except biblical MSS), and other materials. Its purpose is to aid the Qumrân workers to fill in lacunae in their MSS. Caution, however, must be exercised in using such a tool; if the student cannot find what he is looking for in this dictionary, he should not give up the search; when he does find what appears satisfactory, he should by no means feel that his task is over.

Cf. Bib 39 (1958) 376; ZAW 70 (1958) 129; JBL 77 (1958) 269–70; *Book List* (1959) 35–36; TZ 15 (1959) 61–62; JSS 4 (1959) 148; TLZ 84 (1959) 824–25.

128. *Zorell, F.; *Lexicon Hebraicum et Aramaicum Veteris Testamenti* (Rome: Pontificio Istituto Biblico, 1940—). In 1954, the ninth fascicle of this work appeared (śrp—ttgr); a few more Hebrew words and the Aramaic section will complete the dic-

tionary. A notable contribution is the inclusion of the vocabulary of Ben Sira; bibliographical references are more or less up-to-date.

B. Greek

129. Abbott-Smith, G., *A Manual Greek Lexicon of the New Testament* (2nd ed.; Edinburgh: T. and T. Clark, 1929). An older, convenient manual intended for students, which was first issued in 1922. Regarded as "an excellent piece of work" (Eakin) in its time, it must, of course, yield now to Arndt-Gingrich.

Cf. JTS 24 (1922–23) 97; JR 3 (1923) 330–31.

AG 130. Arndt, W. F., and Gingrich, F. W., *A Greek-English Lexicon of the New Testament and Other Early Christian Literature* (A translation and adaptation of Walter Bauer's *Griechisch-Deutsches Wörterbuch zu den Schriften des Neuen Testaments und der übrigen urchristlichen Literatur,* 4th rev. and aug. ed., 1952; Chicago: University of Chicago Press, 1957). Since it is an adaptation as well as a translation of the fourth edition of Bauer's famous Lexicon, it excels it in many ways; but it should be compared with the fifth German edition. Though it is primarily a lexicographical work, its theological importance should not be underestimated.

Cf. Bib 38 (1957) 355–56; ExpTim 68 (1956–57) 262–63; TLZ 82 (1957) 584–85.

131. Bauer, W., *Griechisch-Deutsches Wörterbuch zu den Schriften des Neuen Testaments und der*

übrigen urchristlichen Literatur (5th ed.; Berlin: A. Töpelmann, 1958). A reworking of an older dictionary by E. Preuschen. Its value lies in the attempt to give succinctly the history of the word. It indicates the word's *terminus a quo* in Greek literature, its use in the LXX, papyri, and later Greek as well as the NT occurrences. Abundant bibliographical references to articles and books on the word are also supplied. It is indispensable and is "internationally recognized [as the] best New Testament dictionary."

Cf. TLZ 53 (1928) 541–42; JTS 30 (1928–29) 201; RB 37 (1928) 618–20; ZNW 43 (1950–51) 266.

LS 132. Liddell, H. G., and Scott, R., *A Greek-English Lexicon* (9th ed. by S. Jones and R. McKenzie; 2 vols.; Oxford: Clarendon Press, 1925–40). Though it is a dictionary mainly of classical Greek, it frequently includes LXX and NT usages. It is especially useful for tracing the history of a NT word and for determining its etymology.

Cf. CP 38 (1942) 96–98; JoHellenSt 62 (1942) 94.

MM 133. Moulton, J. H., and Milligan, G., *The Vocabulary of the Greek Testament, Illustrated from the Papyri and Other Non-Literary Sources* (2nd ed.; London: Hodder and Stoughton, 1949). Begun in 1914, the one-volume edition first appeared in 1930. It does not profess to be a complete lexicon to the NT, but lists only those NT words that are found in nonliterary papyri and other nonliterary sources (inscriptions, etc.). It thus attests the ordinary usage of NT words. Since it gives the context of the word's use in the particular text, it is quite indispensable, even though we now have an excellent NT lexicon in Bauer (or Arndt-Gingrich).

Cf. RB 12 (1915) 262–65; TLZ 56 (1931) 223–24; ClR 1 (1931) 530–31.

134. Preisigke, Friedrich, *Wörterbuch der griechischen Papyrusurkunden mit Einschluss der griechischen Inschriften, Aufschriften, Ostraka, Mumienschilder usw. aus Ägypten.* Vollendet und herausgegeben von E. Kiessling (Berlin: Published by the Author, Vol. 1 [1925], 2 [1927], 3 [1931], 4 [1944]). A very important dictionary of the nonliterary Greek texts found in papyri and inscriptions, whose use is absolutely necessary in a thorough study of NT Greek.

Cf. Bib 6 (1925) 482–85; OLZ 34 (1931) 16–18.

135. Schleusner, J. F., *Novus thesaurus philologico-criticus sive Lexicon in Septuaginta et reliquos interpretes Graecos* (3 vols.; London: J. Duncan, 1829). This is the only dictionary of the Greek OT in existence. It still retains some value; most often the student will do better to refer to the latest edition of LS and the various dictionaries of the Greek NT.

136. *Zerwick, M., *Analysis philologica Novi Testamenti Graeci* (Rome: Pontificio Istituto Biblico, 1953). A handy companion to Merk's Greek text, supplying a running vocabulary and the parsing of the NT text together with short exegetical comments. It imitates and improves on F. Rienecker, *Sprachlicher Schlüssel zum griechischen Neuen Testa-*

ment (Giessen: Brunnen-Verlag, 1957). Obviously intended for those who are beginning their study of the NT text, it is not to be regarded as a pretext to eliminate personal research or the consultation of standard grammars and lexica.

Cf. RB 62 (1955) 135; ZKT 76 (1954) 360; CBQ 17 (1955) 108–11.

137. *Zorell, F., *Lexicon Graecum Novi Testamenti* (2nd ed.; Cursus Sacrae Scripturae, pars prior, libri introductorii 7; Paris: Lethielleux, 1931). When it was first published in 1911, it was the only NT lexicon which had made use of the material from the papyri: "a careful compilation quite up to the level of modern research" (Richards). It is a lexicon of the canonical writings only and thus differs from Bauer, which includes early Christian writings. The second edition, which made use of the researches of Preuschen, Bauer, Preisigke, Moulton and Milligan, was highly praised. Unfortunately, it has not been kept up-to-date; yet in many ways it is still quite useful.

Cf. JTS 15 (1914) 87; 33 (1931–32) 297–98; TLZ 56 (1931) 344; OrChr 22 (1931) 249–51.

⋆ VII. Grammars ⋆

A. Hebrew

138. Bauer, H., and Leander, P., *Historische Gram-matik der hebräischen Sprache des Alten Testa-ments* (Vol. 1; Halle: Niemeyer, 1922). The work was to be completed by a second volume; only the first (orthography, phonology, morphology) and an appended set of paradigms appeared. Though recent developments in the study of Hebrew have dated this work, it may still be used cautiously for reference.

139. Beer, G., *Hebräische Grammatik* (2nd ed. rev. by R. Meyer; 2 vols.; Berlin: W. de Gruyter, 1952, 1955). These little volumes are part of the Samm-lung Göschen; though small, they make an excel-lent reference grammar for students who already have some elementary knowledge of Hebrew. The development is along comparative and historical lines; account is taken of Ugaritic and the Qumrân scrolls.
    Cf. RB 61 (1954); 305–6; 63 (1956) 619–20; Bib 35 (1954) 117–21; 38 (1957) 95–98; ArOr 22 (1955) 488 ff.; 24 (1956) 153 ff.; *Eleven Years of Bible Bibliography,* pp. 532, 782.

140. Brockelmann, C., *Hebräische Syntax* (Neukirchen: Verlag der Buchhandlung des Erziehungsvereins,

1956). The plan of this book follows almost section for section that of the author's older comparative syntax, *Grundriss der vergleichenden Grammatik der semitischen Sprachen* (Vol. 2: Syntax, 1913. The work is quite up-to-date and incorporates material from the Hebrew of the Qumrân scrolls. Though a number of points are treated much too briefly, and though a number of views are open to serious debate, this will be a very useful work. There is a very full bibliography.

Cf. ZAW 68 (1956) 265; *Book List* (1957) 73; JSS 2 (1957) 389–91; TLZ 83 (1958) 346–47.

141. Gesenius, W., and Kautzsch, E., *Gesenius' Hebrew Grammar* (tr. by A. E. Cowley; 2nd Eng. ed.; Oxford: Clarendon Press, 1910). The best reference grammar in English.

142. Gesenius, W., *Hebräische Grammatik* (29th ed. rev. by G. Bergsträsser; Part 1 [Leipzig: Vogel, 1918]; Part 2 [Leipzig: Hinrichs, 1929]). Bergsträsser's revision did not touch the syntax. Though it is the most important reference grammar, it needs to be supplemented by modern knowledge of the northwest Semitic language group.

143. *Joüon, P., *Grammaire de l'hébreu biblique* (2nd ed.; Rome: Pontificio Istituto Biblico, 1947). The first edition of this grammar appeared in 1923; this edition is a reprint with correction of typographical errors. Particularly valuable for its treatment of the syntax of the verb. There is a short history of Hebrew grammar (pp. 6–9) which should be consulted for critical evaluation of earlier grammars and dictionaries.

B. Aramaic

144. Bauer, H., and Leander, P., *Grammatik des Bib-lisch-Aramäischen* (Halle: Niemeyer, 1927). This is the standard reference grammar for biblical Aramaic.

C. Greek

145. *Abel, F.-M., *Grammaire du grec biblique suivie d'un choix de papyrus* (Etudes bibliques; Paris: Gabalda, 1927). A grammar of *biblical* Greek, sensibly treating the origin, scope, and character of Koine and making use of the best of Mayser, Deissmann, Thackeray, *et al.* It is intended for students but is a scholarly treatment, based on a thorough knowledge of the Greek of the LXX, the papyri, and the NT. It has long been regarded as the best of French grammars of biblical Greek, but it is now slightly out-of-date.
Cf. JTS 30 (1928–29) 202; Bib 10 (1929) 251–53.

146. Blass, F., and Debrunner, A., *Grammatik des neu-testamentlichen Griechisch* (9th ed.; Göttingen: Vandenhoeck & Ruprecht, 1954). The best NT grammar in small compass, "a classic." "Un ouvrage de première valeur dont l'éloge n'est plus à faire" (Benoit). An English translation, incorporating many of the notes of the late Prof. Debrunner, has been prepared by R. W. Funk of Drew University and is to be published by the University of Chicago Press. The ninth German edition is a little difficult to use, until one gets used to the format,

because of the listing of examples in a fine-print paragraph and an *Anhang;* this has been simplified in the forthcoming English edition. First published in 1896, it has undergone many thorough revisions, the most complete of which was the seventh (1943).

Cf. RB 62 (1955) 447; TLZ 82 (1957) 110–15; HJ 54 (1955–56) 93–94.

147. Burton, E. D., *Syntax of the Moods and Tenses in New Testament Greek* (2nd ed.; Edinburgh: T. and T. Clark, 1894). Old, but in many respects still quite useful. Reprinted 1955.

148. Mayser, E., *Grammatik der griechischen Papyri aus der Ptolemäerzeit: Mit Einschluss der gleichzeitigen Ostraka und der in Ägypten verfassten Inschriften* (2nd ed.; Berlin–Leipzig: W. de Gruyter, Vol. 1/1–2 [1938]; 1/3 [1936]; 2/1 [1926]; 2/2 [1934]; 2/3 [1934]). An indispensable tool for the study of the Greek papyri and for the study of NT Greek as it is reflected in these papyri.

Cf. BS 84 (1927) 234–35; RB 36 (1927) 435–39.

149. Moule, C. F. D., *An Idiom-book of New Testament Greek* (2nd ed.; Cambridge: University Press, 1959). Without pretending to be a thorough and systematic treatment, this book is a readable and useful study of the main features of NT syntax. It is "an attempt to provide a syntactical companion to the interpretation of the NT" (p. vii).

Cf. ExpTim 65 (1953–54) 104; NTS 1 (1954–55) 62–65; JTS n.s. 5 (1954) 243–44; ClR 44 (1959) 752.

150. Moulton, J. H., and Howard, F. W., *A Grammar*

of New Testament Greek (Edinburgh: T. and T. Clark, Vol. 1 [Prolegomena, 3rd ed.] 1949; 2 [Accidence and Word Formation] 1929). A very good grammar, which was unfortunately never completed; Vol. 3 (Syntax), in many ways the most important aspect of NT grammar, has been announced as "In preparation" for years.

Cf. RB 40 (1931) 130–31; ExpTim 41 (1929–30) 113.

151. Radermacher, L., *Neutestamentliche Grammatik: Das Griechisch des Neuen Testaments im Zusammenhang mit der Volkssprache dargestellt* (HNT 1; 2nd ed.; Tübingen: J. C. B. Mohr, 1925). Not a thorough grammar of NT Greek, but "a sort of essay on the *Koinê* in general" (Meillet).

Cf. TLZ 51 (1926) 327–28; RHR 64 (1911) 112–16.

152. Robertson, A. T., *A Grammar of the Greek New Testament in the Light of Historical Research* (4th ed.; London: Hodder and Stoughton, 1923). A vast tome of 1454 pages that treats thoroughly many of the NT grammatical problems. It first appeared in 1914.

Cf. RB 12 (1915) 587–93.

153. Thackeray, H. St. John, *A Grammar of the Old Testament in Greek* (Vol. 1; Cambridge: University Press, 1909). Only this one volume, covering orthography, phonology, and morphology, ever appeared. The grammatical material is drawn almost exclusively from the uncials A, B, S, and a few other uncial MSS which had been collated for Swete's manual edition of the LXX; abundant use was made of the papyri. This work remains the

one indispensable grammar of the Greek OT; it is entirely independent of and superior to the slightly earlier grammar of R. Helbing, *Grammatik der Septuaginta: Laut- und Wortlehre* (Göttingen, 1907), which was too harshly criticized by J. Wackernagel in TLZ 33 (1908) 635 ff. Cf. JTS 11 (1910) 293–300; TR 15 (1912) 352.

154. *Zerwick, M., *Graecitas biblica exemplis illustratur* (3rd ed.; Rome: Pontificio Istituto Biblico, 1955). A compact summary in Latin of NT syntax, which has been highly praised for its good sense and enlightening comments on various passages. Quite useful.

Cf. RB 53 (1946) 473; TLZ 76 (1951) 231–32.

★ VIII. Concordances ★

155. Lisowsky, G., *Konkordanz zum hebräischen Alten Testament* (Stuttgart: Württembergische Bibelanstalt, 1958). A handy concordance to Kittel's Hebrew Bible; it is reproduced from a hand copy which is not always too easy to read. Only nouns and verbs are given full coverage, though all the words in the Hebrew dictionaries are mentioned, and the proper names are given with mere reference to where they appear. The words are translated into German, English (according to the meanings in BDB), and Latin (classical, not Vulgate). Though useful as a handy reference, it could never supplant Mandelkern.

156. Mandelkern, S., *Veteris Testamenti concordantiae Hebraicae atque Chaldaicae* (new printing; 2 vols.; Graz: Akademische Druck und Verlagsanstalt, 1955). The work originally appeared in 1896; in 1925, a second enlarged edition was issued. M. H. Goshen-Gottstein has published a third edition with corrections and supplements (Jerusalem–Tel Aviv: Schocken, 1956, 1959). Indispensable.

157. Hatch, E., and Redpath, H. A., *A Concordance to the Septuagint* (new printing; 2 vols.; Graz: Akademische Druck und Verlagsanstalt). First published in 1897 in two volumes; a third, supple-

mentary volume appeared in 1906. The aim is to present a complete concordance to the Greek version of the OT, to the deuterocanonical books (Apocrypha), and to the remains of the other versions contained in the Hexapla. The work is based on the uncials ABSR. An attempt is made to indicate what words of the MT are being translated by the Greek. There is a separate treatment of proper names, and a reverse index from Hebrew to Greek. While this work remains an indispensable tool, considerable caution must be exercised in its use. The student must remember that the evidence is limited to four MSS; he ought not blindly to accept the equivalences between Greek and Hebrew; after finding his references, he must have recourse to the large editions of the LXX for any variants.

158. Bruder, C. H., *Tamieion tôn tês kainês Diathêkês lexeôn sive Concordantiae omnium vocum Novi Testamenti Graeci* (4th ed.; Leipzig: E. Bredt, 1888). An old concordance to the Greek NT, which was based originally on the Textus Receptus and enriched in subsequent editions with readings from the critical studies of Tregelles, Westcott-Hort, Tischendorf, and Lachmann. It has, however, been superseded in more recent times by that of Moulton and Geden.

159. Moulton, W. F., and Geden, A. S., *A Concordance to the Greek Testament according to the Texts of Westcott and Hort, Tischendorf and the English*

Revisers (3rd ed.; Edinburgh: T. and T. Clark, 1926; reprinted 1950). Issued for the first time in 1897, it aimed at providing a concordance to the text of the NT found in modern critical editions and replacing the former standard work of C. H. Bruder, which was based on the Textus Receptus. It is a complete concordance based first of all on Westcott-Hort and compared with the other two texts mentioned in the title; marginal readings are also included. Indispensable.

160. Schmoller, A., *Handkonkordanz zum griechischen Neuen Testament (Text nach Nestle)* (9th ed.; Stuttgart: Württembergische Bibelanstalt, 1951). An excellent, handy, and cheap one-volume concordance to the NT Greek text. But it is not a complete concordance. The articles on words which are very common have been abridged. It indicates whether the word occurs in the LXX and also gives the Latin equivalent of the Vulgate. Quite useful, but for an exhaustive study one must consult Moulton and Geden.

Cf. NRT 67 (1945) 472–73; RevScRel 20 (1940) 427–28.

161. Smith, J. B., *Greek-English Concordance to the New Testament: A Tabular and Statistical Greek-English Concordance, Based on the King James Version with an English to Greek Index* (Scottdale, Pa.: Mennonite Publishing House, 1955). Useful, even though the texts used are the King James version and the Textus Receptus of R. Estienne

(1550)! It lists the number of times the Greek word occurs in its various meanings.

Cf. VD 34 (1956) 311–12; RB 64 (1957) 611–12; CBQ 18 (1956) 457–58.

162. *Peultier, E., Etienne, L., and Gantois, L., *Concordantiarum universae sacrae Scripturae thesaurus* (2nd ed.; Paris: Lethielleux, 1939). This is a corrected impression of the 1897 edition.

★ IX. Introductions to the Bible ★

A. Common

163. *Robert, A., and Feuillet, A. (edd.), *Introduction à la Bible* (2 vols.; Tournai: Desclée, Vol. 1 [Introduction générale. Ancien Testament], 2nd ed., 1959; Vol. 2 [Nouveau Testament], 1959). Though not intended for a strictly scholarly audience, this is the best informed and most modern Catholic introduction to the OT and NT. The first volume originally appeared in 1957.

   Cf. ETL 31 (1958) 381–83; CBQ 20 (1958) 246–48; RB 65 (1958) 437–38; OLZ 53 (1958) 450–52; *Scripture* 10 (1958) 62–63; ZAW 70 (1958) 130; *Book List* (1958) 29.

164. *Robert, A., and Tricot, A. (edd.), *Initiation biblique* (3rd ed.; Tournai: Desclée, 1954). This work was first issued in 1939; in 1948, a revised and expanded edition was published. A third French edition, revised and augmented with nearly one hundred pages of new material, was published. This volume contains more than general and special introduction to the OT and NT; there are essays on geography, history, archaeology, theology, languages, etc. An English version, *Guide to the Bible,* by E. P. Arbez and M. R. P. McGuire, has appeared (Vol. 1, 2nd ed.; New York: Desclée, 1960. This is a very useful manual for the student.

   Cf. RSR 43 (1955) 451–52; TLZ 80 (1955) 207–9; RB

63 (1956) 280–81; *Eleven Years of Bible Bibliography*, pp. 227, 715–16.

B. OT

165. Anderson, B. W., *Understanding the Old Testament* (Englewood Cliffs, N.J.: Prentice-Hall, 1957). This survey of the history and religion of Israel is particularly recommended for college students and seminarians. It sets the biblical writings into their historical background. Archaeological data and the best modern literature are excellently used; there are maps, chronological charts, over sixty illustrations, and a bibliography of supplementary readings limited to English titles.

Cf. JSS 3 (1958) 83; *Book List* (1958) 25; *Interpretation* 12 (1958) 244–48; CBQ 20 (1958) 390–92.

166. Bentzen, A., *Introduction to the Old Testament* (2 vols.; 2nd ed.; Copenhagen: Gad, 1952). This work appeared originally in Danish (1941); a revised and rewritten English translation was issued in 1948. In 1952, a second English edition was published, incorporating additional material in appendices; subsequent "editions" are reprints of the second. The deuterocanonical (apocryphal) and pseudepigraphical books are included. The work is particularly valuable for the discussion of the forms of OT literature and the presentation of Scandinavian views.

Cf. JBL 67 (1948) 399–402; TLZ 75 (1950) 541–45; BO 7 (1950) 183–85; Bib 32 (1951) 276–80; *Eleven Years of Bible Bibliography*, pp. 23, 195, 495.

[54]

167. Driver, S. R., *An Introduction to the Literature of the Old Testament* (9th ed.; Edinburgh: T. and T. Clark, 1913). This is the latest revision. In spite of its age, this work still retains great value.

168. Eissfeldt, O., *Einleitung in das Alte Testament* (2nd ed.; Tübingen: J. C. B. Mohr, 1956). A revised and greatly expanded form of the first edition (1934). Nearly one quarter of the book is devoted to the preliterary materials and to the literary prehistory of the OT books. There are detailed introductions to each of the books, including the deuterocanonical (apocryphal) and pseudepigraphical books, and the Qumrân scrolls. The bibliographies are rich. This is the best modern introduction to the OT.

   Cf. CBQ 19 (1957) 529–30; TLZ 82 (1957) 681–82; TZ 13 (1957) 300–303; *Book List* (1957) 36–37; ArOr 26 (1958) 520–23; Bib 39 (1958) 231–32; JTS n.s. 9 (1958) 113–14; RB 65 (1958) 119–21; JBL 77 (1958) 258–59; RSPT 42 (1958) 143–45; BZ (1959) 107–12.

169. Gottwald, N. K., *A Light to the Nations* (New York: Harper, 1959). A survey of the OT resembling very much in plan, extent, and purpose the work of Anderson, though in many details it presents a different viewpoint. There is a wealth of illustration and a bibliography of English titles for supplementary reading.

   Cf. TS 21 (1960) 136–38; JSS 5 (1960) 87–88.

170. Hempel, J., *Althebräische Literatur und ihr hellenistisch-jüdisches Nachleben* (Wildpark–Potsdam: Akademische Verlagsgesellschaft Athenaion, 1930–

34). Part of a series, *Handbuch der Literaturwissenschaft,* edited by O. Walzel, this work surveys the literary development from the earliest songs and poems through the Persian and Greek period to Philo, Josephus, and the Gospels. After a brief statement of preliminaries on geography, ethnology, etc., the forms of literature are analyzed, Oriental parallels cited, and the peculiar contribution of Israel indicated; the second half treats of Israelite literature as part of national history. Though one of the earliest attempts to write a history of Israelite-Jewish literature, this work still remains a very valuable reference tool.

Cf. JTS 36 (1935) 441–42; JPOS 15 (1935) 344–45; TLZ 61 (1936) 119–23; Bib 17 (1936) 116–20.

171. Lods, A., *Histoire de la littérature hébraïque et juive* (Paris: Payot, 1950). A posthumous work, edited by A. Parrot, who added a chapter on the Qumrân scrolls. This is a gigantic attempt to write a history of Israelite-Jewish literature, including deuterocanonical (apocryphal) and pseudepigraphical books, and other materials, from the earliest times to the revolt of 135 A.D.; books and parts of books are arranged in the order in which Lods thought they were written. The author was a good Hebraist and well acquainted with the Bible; he lacked, however, control of other Semitic languages and familiarity with archaeology, and his views are those of the literary critics at the turn of the century. The book has value but must be used with great caution.

Cf. RB 57 (1950) 402–4; *Eleven Years of Bible Bibliography,* pp. 261–62.

172. Pfeiffer, R. H., *History of New Testament Times* (New York: Harper, 1949). The title may be misleading, since the book is not a history of Christian NT times. There is a survey of the political, religious, and literary history of Palestinian and Alexandrian Judaism, which extends mainly from the Maccabean revolt to Bar Kokhba; at least half the book is devoted to introduction to the apocryphal books. This is a very useful handbook, particularly for the statement of problems and the surveys of opinions; the author gives his own views, which will not always be shared by scholars. The bibliography is very full.

Cf. *Eleven Years of Bible Bibliography,* pp. 262–63; CBQ 12 (1950) 474–75; *Interpretation* 4 (1950) 93–95; JBL 69 (1950) 67–69; RB 59 (1952) 267–71.

173. Pfeiffer, R. H., *Introduction to the Old Testament* (New York: Harper, 1941). This is a large introduction, packed with information and references to literature of all ages. The author was well acquainted with the trends of his time but, though trying to find a middle course, tended in many ways to be much more radical than biblical scholars would be today. The book is valuable for extensive coverage of the material, references to the literature, and as a "landmark."

Cf. JBL 61 (1942) 111–26; BO 8 (1953) 150–57.

174. Torrey, C. C., *The Apocryphal Literature: A Short Introduction* (New Haven: Yale University Press, 1945). This small work contains a general introduction to questions of the Apocrypha (deuterocanonical books) and special introductions to each of the

books; two books, which have never been considered among the Apocrypha, are included here, scil., *The Lives of the Prophets* and *The Testament of Job*. The book is critical and always original.

Cf. *Eleven Years of Bible Bibliography,* p. 30; JBL 65 (1946) 217–21; JTS 48 (1947) 211–15.

175. Weiser, A., *Einleitung in das Alte Testament* (4th ed.; Göttingen: Vandenhoeck & Ruprecht, 1957). Originally published in 1939, this work was issued in a second revised edition (1949) which included sections on the deuterocanonical (apocryphal) and pseudepigraphical books. The third edition was unchanged, but the fourth is an extensive revision which contains about twenty pages on the Qumrân scrolls and up-to-date bibliographies. Though much shorter than the work of Eissfeldt, which it resembles in organization, this is an excellent handy introduction.

Cf. TLZ 75 (1950) 545–46; TS 11 (1950) 413–16; Bib 32 (1951) 273–76; BZ 3 (1959) 112–17; *Eleven Years of Bible Bibliography,* p. 30; *Book List* (1958) 30.

C. NT

176. Feine, P., and Behm, J., *Einleitung in das Neue Testament* (9th ed.; Heidelberg: Quelle und Meyer, 1950). One of the best introductions to the NT, characterized by solid scholarship and a sane, but not too conservative, approach. Little use is made, however, of Catholic studies, though some are mentioned in the bibliographies.

Cf. RB 46 (1937) 453–55; Bib 20 (1939) 95–99; JTS 38 (1937) 273–74.

177. *Gaechter, P., *Summa introductionis in Novum Testamentum* (Innsbruck–Leipzig: F. Rauch, 1938). A brief and concise exposé of the principal literary questions concerning the NT, written in Latin for students. Outmoded on the Synoptic question, sketchy on the Epistles, but nevertheless useful.

    Cf. RSR 29 (1939) 365–67; ETL 16 (1939) 128; ThRev 38 (1939) 261–62; Bib 20 (1939) 217–20.

178. Goguel, M., *Introduction au Nouveau Testament* (4 vols.; Paris: Leroux, 1922–27). The standard French introduction of almost encyclopedic scope. It contains many good points and sane discussions together with some that are rather peculiar and certainly outmoded.

    Cf. RB 31 (1922) 443–49; 33 (1924) 128–30, 605–11; 34 (1925) 446–48; 36 (1927) 579–84; JR 2 (1922) 651–52; 4 (1924) 102–3; 5 (1925) 553–54; 7 (1927) 472–74.

179. Henshaw, T., *New Testament Literature in the Light of Modern Scholarship* (London: Allen and Unwin, 1952). "Not intended for specialist theological students, but for others to whom biblical study is one of several main subjects." Nevertheless, it offers a good summary of the results of modern scholarship in the NT field.

    Cf. ExpTim 64 (1952) 9–10.

180. Lake, K., and Lake, S., *An Introduction to the New Testament* (New York: Harper, 1937). A well-balanced and critical treatment of the NT books, not in chronological order but as they occur in the canon, together with excursus on Jewish and Greek

backgrounds of the NT. There are many penetrating observations and stimulating proposals in the book. Useful appendices treat NT chronology and topography. The section on John is somewhat weak.

Cf. JR 18 (1938) 315–17; ExpTim 49 (1937–38) 353; HJ 36 (1937–38) 295.

181. McNeile, A. H., *An Introduction to the Study of the New Testament* (2nd ed. rev. by C. S. C. Williams; Oxford: Clarendon Press, 1953). A good, standard NT introduction, first published in 1927, now reworked and brought up-to-date. The new section on Form Criticism contains seven points of criticism that must not be overlooked. The book was not written for specialists but for students at Oxford.

Cf. ExpTim 64 (1952-53) 363–64; RB 61 (1954) 276–77.

182. *Meinertz, M., *Einleitung in das Neue Testament* (5th ed.; Paderborn: F. Schöningh, 1950). A less detailed but somewhat conservative introduction written by a well-known Catholic exegete. The fourth edition was a complete reworking of an older *Einleitung* by A. Schaefer (first published 1898), of which only the framework remains in the fourth and fifth editions.

Cf. TS 11 (1950) 411–13; NRT 61 (1934) 307–8; 72 (1950) 532–33; ZKT 72 (1950) 499–500.

183. Michaelis, W., *Einleitung in das Neue Testament* (2nd ed.; Bern: B. Haller, 1954). A very good and very thorough NT introduction by a reputable

Swiss scholar. Though he at times expresses a very personal view on a problem, he is careful to give an accurate résumé of the opinions of others and a searching analysis of them.

Cf. ZNW 45 (1954) 275–76; RB 63 (1956) 138–39.

184. *Wikenhauser, A., *New Testament Introduction* (tr. by Joseph Cunningham; New York: Herder and Herder, 1958). A translation of *Einleitung in das Neue Testament* (2nd ed.; Freiburg: Herder, 1956). By far the best Catholic introduction to the NT. It is similar to Feine-Behm in many ways. The essay on Form Criticism has been praised as excellent, open-minded, and displaying sound judgment.

Cf. JTS n.s. 4 (1953) 228–29; RB 61 (1954) 274–76; ZKT 75 (1953) 478–82; TS 14 (1953) 602–6; 20 (1959) 114–16.

★ X. Commentaries in Series ★

A. Common

CHS 185. *A Catholic Commentary on Holy Scripture*. Published in London in 1953 under the editorship of E. F. Sutcliffe for the OT and B. Orchard for the NT. Most of this volume is the work of British and Irish scholars, with some contributions from North America. No translation is printed, but the commentary supposes use of the Douay-Rheims version; there are a number of introductory articles for both Testaments. The tone of the work is extremely conservative; there are a few valuable items in the book. The student will not generally profit by using this volume.

Cf. RB 64 (1957) 598–601; TLZ 83 (1958) 671–73.

EB 186. *Etudes bibliques*. A series published by Gabalda of Paris, which was begun by M.-J. Lagrange and is continued under the direction of the Ecole Biblique de Jérusalem. The series contains not only commentaries on books of the OT and NT but also many learned and useful monographs on Palestinian history, geography, and archaeology. The NT commentaries in this series are very thorough; those of Rigaux (on Thess) and Spicq (on Heb and Past) are the "last word." Dhorme's commentary on Job is still a classic, and Abel's commentary on Maccabees is presently the best.

[63]

ICC 187. *The International Critical Commentary.* Began to appear in 1895 under the direction of C. A. Briggs, S. R. Driver, and A. Plummer. It was intended to supply the English reader with a commentary on both Testaments which would be comparable to the German critical works of the time. When Montgomery's commentary on Kings was published in 1951, the series was far from finished. In keeping with the plan, the emphasis is critical and philological. Naturally, the quality of production is uneven, and many of the volumes are much dated; but some of the contributions (e.g., of Driver, Moore, Montgomery, Sanday-Headlam, Burton, Plummer) retain their value.

IB 188. *The Interpreter's Bible.* Began to appear in 1952, with G. A. Buttrick as editor of the commentary. The series, covering both Testaments, is complete in twelve volumes. For each biblical book, the King James and RSV translations are printed in parallel columns; there are extensive introductions and commentaries, and sections of homiletic exposition; over half of Vol. 1 and Vol. 7 is devoted to extensive essays on OT and NT background. Though the contributions vary considerably in quality and viewpoint, one will still find a good deal of excellent material in these volumes. The biblical student can profitably ignore the expositions.

BJ 189. **La sainte Bible.* Began to appear in fascicles in 1948 under the direction of the Ecole Biblique de Jérusalem; hence the work is often called *Bible de Jérusalem.* The series, covering both Testaments, was completed in 1954; it contains a critical translation from the original languages, introductions of moderate length, and notes. In 1956, a single-volume edition was issued, in which the notes were telescoped and the introductions abbreviated. A second, revised edition in fascicle form, with restored introductions and notes, has been appearing since 1957 and will soon be completed. The contributions differ somewhat in quality, but on the whole the authors present the best of modern biblical scholarship. This Bible is highly recommended.

190. *La sainte Bible.* Began to appear in 1935 from Paris under the editorship of L. Pirot, who was succeeded by A. Clamer. The commentary, in twelve volumes, covers both Testaments; all has been published except the Minor Prophets. Both the Vulgate and a translation from the original languages is printed. Both the quality and bulk of the various volumes differ; the more recent ones are quite extensive in introduction and comment, and represent great advances in Catholic biblical scholarship. Some of the work, e.g., Exodus, can be used very profitably.

B. OT

ATD 191. *Das Alte Testament Deutsch.* Began to appear in 1949 from Göttingen under the editorship of V. Herntrich and A. Weiser. Twenty-five volumes of moderate size are planned; Vol. 1 is Weiser, *Einleitung in das Alte Testament* (see Introductions). About two thirds of the work has been published, and a couple of volumes (notably Weiser's on the Psalms) have been revised. The commentary is presented in running—almost essay—form, with a minimum of philology and great emphasis on theology. Some well-known German biblical scholars have contributed (e.g., Weiser, Noth, von Rad, Elliger, Eichrodt). Though not intended for the specialist, this is a very useful commentary.

192. *La Bible: L'Ancien Testament.* In two volumes (1956, 1959) under the editorship of E. Dhorme. This work, most of which comes from the editor himself, has a new critical translation, introductions, and notes, and includes the deuterocanonical books. Scholarship and sobriety of judgment characterize these volumes, which obviously invite comparison with the *Bible de Jérusalem.* Though intended for the layman, the work can be used with great profit by the student.

BK 193. *Biblischer Kommentar: Altes Testament.* Began to appear in 1955 from Neukirchen under the general editorship of M. Noth. The work is to be completed in about 120 fascicles (nearly ten thousand pages); so far, about one tenth, mostly on Psalms, is finished. The editor and his collaborators make a list of formidable names. The series is intended as a great scientific commentary of critical, philological, and theological interest; in place of the older, narrow literary criticism, tradition-history and Form Criticism play a dominant part. Though criticism in detail is inevitable, the published fascicles have been warmly received by reviewers. Highly recommended as a reference work.

CaB 194. *The Cambridge Bible for Schools and Colleges.* Began to appear in 1880 under the general direction of J. Perowne, who was succeeded by A. F. Kirkpatrick. The series is complete and includes a volume of introduction to the Pentateuch and commentaries on 1 Maccabees, Wisdom, and Ben Sira. Many of the volumes have undergone several revisions, and some were replaced by the works of new authors. The series is intended for popular use, and in this category it still contains some of the best commentaries in English. On the whole, it is a very sober work; the introductions are quite extensive and, though dated, still have much of value.

Cf. ExpTim 71 (1959) 4–7.

195. Fritzsche, O., and Grimm, C., *Kurzgefasstes exegetisches Handbuch zu den Apokryphen des Alten Testaments* (6 vols.; Leipzig: Hirzel, 1851–60). In many respects this great commentary has not been surpassed. It still remains a very important reference work.

AT 196. *Göttinger Handkommentar zum Alten Testament.* Began to appear in 1892 under the editorship of W. Nowack. The series was completed, but a number of volumes were being revised into the 1920's; in 1926, Gunkel's volume on the Psalms replaced Bäthgen's. Some of the authors were among the most radical of the German critics of the last century; though many of the views were rejected by sober scholars in the past—and more so in the present—this work still remains the monument to German biblical scholarship at the end of the nineteenth and in the first decade of the twentieth century. The commentary is still important for the biblical scholar.

HAT 197. *Handbuch zum Alten Testament.* Began to appear in 1943 from Tübingen under the editorship of O. Eissfeldt. Though the series is still far from complete, several volumes have undergone revision, and Bertholet's commentary on Ezekiel has been replaced by Fohrer's. Two sections are planned—the first on the books of the Hebrew canon, the other on the deuterocanonical (apocryphal) and pseudepigraphical books; of the second section, the commentary on Wisdom has appeared. A good deal of the best modern German scholarship and a variety of critical views are represented here; the commentary is compact, with emphasis on the philological.

HS 198. **Die heilige Schrift des Alten Testaments.* Began to
or appear in 1923 from Bonn under the editorship of
BB F. Feldmann and H. Herkenne. The series is complete, except for the volume on Ezra–Nehemiah; a few supplementary volumes have been issued. The introductions are quite extensive, and the commentary is very full. Naturally, the quality of the different volumes varies, as do also the tendencies of the different authors. Some parts are well worth consulting. It is often referred to as the *Bonnerbibel.*

199. Wace, H. (ed.), *The Holy Bible . . . Apocrypha* (2 vols.; London: J. Murray, 1888). These volumes form part of the so-called *Speaker's Commentary* on the complete Bible. The English version of 1611

is printed, and the commentary is based on it. The introductions and notes are critical. There is still much of value in these volumes.

C. NT

NTC 200. *Black's New Testament Commentaries.* This is a new series, begun in 1957, of English commentaries on the NT, whose general editor is Henry Chadwick; it is published in England by A. and C. Black, London, and in the U.S.A. by Harper (American title: *Harper's New Testament Commentaries*). The purpose of the series is not a detailed critical and textual discussion of the NT, but rather an understanding of the text for the reader who does not know Greek. The list of contributors contains many of the best-known British and American NT scholars. To date Matthew, Luke, Acts, Romans, and Philippians have appeared.

GTC 201. *Cambridge Greek Testament Commentary.* A new series begun in 1955 under the general editorship of C. F. D. Moule and published by the Cambridge University Press. It is intended to replace the old *Cambridge Bible for Schools* and the *Cambridge Greek Testament for Schools and Colleges.* Whereas the old series emphasized the questions of authenticity, history, and philology, the aim of the new series is a theological commentary based on the foundation of sane historical and linguistic study. Space is given in the introduction to the religious ideas in each book. To date two volumes have appeared: Colossians and Philemon (Moule),

Mark (Cranfield). Though small in scope, they are a good starting point for the study of the Greek text.

CNT 202. *Commentaire du Nouveau Testament.* Published under the direction of P. Bonnard, O. Cullmann, *et al.,* by Delachaux et Niestlé, Neuchâtel and Paris. The series began in 1949. Though fifteen volumes are projected, only seven (on nine Epistles of Paul and Hebrews) have appeared so far. It is an up-to-date French Protestant series, which is often quite good, though the individual commentaries are not all of equal value.

HNT 203. *Handbuch zum Neuen Testament.* Founded by H. Lietzmann in 1906, it is now edited by G. Bornkamm and published by J. C. B. Mohr, Tübingen. There are twenty-three volumes, which are undergoing a revision or complete rewriting. The comments are short, normally of a critical and philological nature, and usually supply copious material from the comparative study of religions. They are compact and very informative volumes. Highly recommended.

HThK 204. **Herders Theologischer Kommentar zum Neuen Testament.* A new series begun by A. Wikenhauser in 1953, published by Herder, Freiburg. A series of fourteen volumes is projected, aiming at a detailed, strictly scientific commentary on the NT for Catholic readers. Its title indicates its avowed aim: to treat the theological character of the NT books, without in the least neglecting the critical, textual, philological, archaeological, or historical problems which may be connected with the text. To date only one volume has appeared (13, fasc. 3: *Die Johannesbriefe,* by R. Schnackenburg—a very auspicious beginning).

eyer 205. *Kritisch-exegetischer Kommentar über das Neue Testament.* Founded by H. A. W. Meyer, after whom it is often called the *Meyerkommentar,* it was begun in 1832; it is published by Vandenhoeck & Ruprecht, Göttingen. The series of sixteen volumes has often been revised and even completely rewritten at times. Composed by the best German Protestant scholars, they offer a thorough critical approach to the NT. It is unquestionably the best series of German commentaries. Since the last war a revision or complete rewriting of the volumes has been under way.

NTD 206. *Das Neue Testament Deutsch.* Edited by P. Althaus and J. Behm, this series was begun in 1912 under the title *Neues Göttinger Bibelwerk.* The fifth edition (1949–50) contains twelve volumes and was published by Vandenhoeck & Ruprecht, Göttingen. Though it is rather conservative in its approach, it attempts to bring out the religious meaning of the NT text. Quite useful.

RNT 207. **Regensburger Neues Testament.* Ten volumes edited by A. Wikenhauser and O. Kuss, published by Pustet, Regensburg. It does not aim to be a commentary for specialists, but rather for the educated reader. As such, it is highly recommended, especially in the new editions of the volumes which have been issued in the last few years. It is certainly the best NT commentary available on this level written by Catholic scholars. The volumes on the Synoptic Gospels (by J. Schmid) are especially recommended.

ThHK 208. *Theologischer Handkommentar zum Neuen Testament.* This series was begun in 1928 but was never completed. A new start has been made, and the publication is being cared for by the Evangelische Verlagsanstalt, Berlin. Vol. 2 (*Das Evangelium nach Markus*) and Vol. 9 (*Der Brief des Paulus an die Galater*) have appeared.

VS 209. **Verbum salutis.* An excellent series of short French commentaries, consisting of sixteen volumes, begun by J. Huby and published by Beauchesne, Paris. A new edition, revising the volumes which are now out-of-date, has been undertaken by S. Lyonnet. The volumes are not all of equal value; the best of them came from the pen of Huby himself. The old edition of the four Gospels in this series was translated into English by J. J. Heenan, *The Word of Salvation* (2 vols.; Milwaukee: Bruce, 1957).

Cf. also the entries under *Intertestamental Period.*

* XI. Dictionaries *

210. Allmen, J. J. von, *Vocabulary of the Bible* (London: Lutterworth Press, 1958). A translation of the French and Swiss Protestant work, *Vocabulaire biblique* (2nd ed.; Neuchâtel: Delachaux et Niestlé, 1956). Thirty-seven scholars have collaborated in the study of 160 key-words which have special significance for NT study. It is planned for students, is clearly written, and avoids Greek and Hebrew terms. It is, however, of uneven quality because of the collaborative effort.
   Cf. CBQ 19 (1957) 269–70; JR 36 (1956) 130; RevScRel 31 (1957) 185–86; TLZ 81 (1956) 545–47.

TW 211. *Bauer, J. B. (ed.), *Bibeltheologisches Wörterbuch* (Graz: Styria, 1958). An excellent biblical theological dictionary in which forty well-known European exegetes (representing six nations) have collaborated. It is intended for theologians and those in the pastoral ministry. Signed articles end with a short bibliography and give an adequate treatment of the most important OT and NT concepts.
   Cf. VD 37 (1959) 119–20.

DBS 212. *Cazelles, H. (ed.), *Dictionnaire de la Bible: Supplément* (Paris: Letouzey et Ané, 1928—). The biblical dictionary of Vigouroux in four volumes

(1895–1912) was very much out-of-date. Instead of attempting a revision, L. Pirot began in 1928 the work of issuing supplementary volumes; after his death, A. Robert became the editor, and in 1956 he was in turn succeeded by Cazelles. So far, five volumes have been published, and the sixth is appearing in fascicles. Many of the articles are as long as monographs, and some are book size; references to the literature are abundant. Naturally, some of the earlier articles are in need of revision, but this monumental work is indispensable to the biblical scholar.

213. Davis, J. D. (ed.), *The Westminster Dictionary of the Bible* (5th ed. rev. and rewritten by H. S. Gehman; Philadelphia: Westminster Press, 1944). The viewpoint is generally conservative; the factual material is accurate, though the identifications of places must be checked in the more recent atlases. A useful handbook.

Cf. *Eleven Years of Bible Bibliography,* p. 3; JBL 64 (1945) 555–58.

214. Galling, K., *Biblisches Reallexikon* (Tübingen: J. C. B. Mohr, 1937). This is the first volume in Eissfeldt's HAT (cf. Commentaries). The *realia* of the Bible are covered adequately and competently; there are 135 illustrations, and each article is supplied with references to the literature. This is a very useful handbook, highly recommended.

Cf. ZDPV 60 (1937) 246–48; OLZ 41 (1938) 538–40; JBL 57 (1938) 234; TLZ 63 (1938) 355–56; JPOS 18 (1938) 133–35.

RGG 215. Galling, K. (ed.), *Die Religion in Geschichte und Gegenwart* (3rd ed.; Tübingen: J. C. B. Mohr, 1957–). A second edition of this standard reference work appeared in 1927–32; the present edition is new and completely revised. There are numerous articles of great importance for students of both Testaments. So far, three volumes have appeared.

216. *Haag, H. (ed.), *Bibel-Lexikon* (Einsiedeln–Zurich: Benziger, 1951). Though this work is dated 1951, the last fascicle did not appear until 1956. The German edition is based on the Dutch biblical dictionary issued in 1941 under the editorship of A. van den Born; there has been extensive revision, and references to the literature have been brought up to date. While the articles are generally short, an abundance of cross references is supplied by which they can be supplemented. Highly recommended.

Cf. *Eleven Years of Bible Bibliography,* pp. 375–76; *Book List* (1957) 7; ZAW 68 (1956) 261–63; CBQ 19 (1957) 132–33; RB 64 (1957) 115.

HDB 217. Hastings, J. (ed.), *A Dictionary of the Bible* (5 vols.; New York: Scribner, 1898–1904). The dictionary proper is contained in the first four volumes; the fifth volume is supplementary and contains articles, index, and maps. Later issues are simply reprints. Though now quite old, this dictionary can still be profitably consulted.

VNT 218. Kittel, G. (ed.), *Theologisches Wörterbuch zum Neuen Testament* (Stuttgart: W. Kohlhammer, 1933–). This work, which was begun by G. Kittel and has been produced with the collaboration of many scholars, represents the best of German NT scholarship of the last twenty-five years. The meanings of NT words are studied historically: after a discussion of the etymology of a word its usage in classical Greek, Hellenistic Greek, the Greek of the Septuagint and of Jewish writers is sketched as a background for the discussion of its use in the NT. When the word has a Hebrew counterpart in the OT, an adequate treatment is also given of the Hebrew word. Stress is put on the semantic and theological development in the history of the word. The work appears periodically in fascicles, and six volumes have already been issued (up to *satanas*). Absolutely indispensable for any serious work in the NT.

219. Klauser, T. (ed.), *Reallexikon für Antike und Christentum: Sachwörterbuch zur Auseinandersetzung des Christentums mit der antiken Welt* (Stuttgart: Hiersemann, 1950—). This important dictionary began to appear during the War, but Vol. 1 was not completed until 1950; since then, two other volumes have been published, and a fourth is in preparation. As the subtitle indicates, the work is a survey of pre-Christian and Christian antiquity, with recognition of their continuity and their difference. Many well-known scholars have contributed articles which are of great value for the student of the OT and NT.

220. Miller, M. S. and J. L., *Harper's Bible Dictionary* (New York: Harper, 1952). Though the authors are responsible for most of the items in this dic-

tionary, a few others have contributed. The Millers sought the advice of experts for their articles, and the result is a generally good work. The user must be warned, however, that he will meet with contradictory statements in the book. Useful for handy reference, but must be checked.

Cf. *Eleven Years of Bible Bibliography,* p. 462; JBL 72 (1953) 194–95; Bib 36 (1955) 87–89.

PW
or
RE

221. *Paulys Real-Encyclopädie der classischen Alter-tumswissenschaft.* Neue Bearbeitung unter Mitwirkung zahlreicher Fachgenossen, herausgegeben von Georg Wissowa (Stuttgart: J. B. Metzler). Commonly referred to as Pauly-Wissowa, this work first appeared in the new edition in 1893. It is not yet complete, and since 1949 there is a new publisher, Alfred Druckenmueller. The system of numbering the volumes is a little confusing. The first series is to contain articles on subjects A–Q (so far it is up to Vol. 23 in this series, to "Pyramiden"); the second series covers R–Z and was begun in 1914 (so far it is up to Vol. 8, to "Vindeleia"). But from time to time *Supplementbände* have appeared to give new or additional material in the letters already published (to date, eight volumes). There are many articles in this dictionary that touch on biblical material, especially that of the late Jewish and NT periods.

* XII. Biblical Theology *

A. Common

221a.*Guillet, J., *Thèmes bibliques* (2nd ed.; Paris: Aubier, 1954). Though not a complete biblical theology, this is a valuable little book which traces such themes as the Exodus, grace-justice-truth, sin, damnation, etc., through the OT and NT. The themes are sometimes sketched rather than developed at length.

Cf. Bib 32 (1951) 319-20; RB 58 (1951) 453-54; TS 12 (1951) 295-97; VT 1 (1951) 235-37; CBQ 14 (1952) 195-99; *Eleven Years of Bible Bibliography*, p. 352.

B. OT

222. Dentan, R. C., *Preface to Old Testament Theology* (New Haven: Yale University Press, 1950). A serious inquiry into what should be the character and method of OT theology. Ultimately, he suggests that the outline of systematic theology, scil., the nature of God, the nature of man, the nature of salvation, will prove best.

Cf. JBL 69 (1950) 393-97; JTS n.s. 2 (1951) 85-86; *Eleven Years of Bible Bibliography*, p. 350.

223. Eichrodt, W., *Theologie des Alten Testaments* (Part 1 [5th ed.; Stuttgart: Klotz; Göttingen: Vandenhoeck & Ruprecht, 1957]; Parts 2-3 [2nd ed.;

[79]

Berlin: Evangelische Verlagsanstalt, 1948]). This is still the classical work of OT theology. The presentation is essentially historical, but a unifying theme is found in the idea of the covenant; the material is arranged under the headings: God and the people; God and the world; God and man. Into the new edition of Part 1 new notes have been introduced to give the author's views on questions currently under discussion.

Cf. Bib 38 (1957) 470–73; *Book List* (1958) 32–33.

224. *Imschoot, P. van, *Théologie de l'Ancien Testament* (2 vols.; Tournai: Desclée, 1954, 1956). This work is to be completed in three volumes; so far, Vol. 1 (God) and Vol. 2 (Man) have appeared. Though aware of development and the variety of views represented in the Bible, the author has been much influenced by the outline of dogmatic theology. The vast amount of material collected and sifted and the bibliographical references will be very valuable to the student.

Cf. TLZ 80 (1955) 275–76; 82 (1957) 850–51; RSR 43 (1955) 403–4; 45 (1957) 100–102; RB 63 (1956) 136–37; 65 (1958) 293–94; *Eleven Years of Bible Bibliography,* pp. 683–84; *Book List* (1957) 46.

225. Jacob, E., *Theology of the Old Testament* (tr. by A. W. Heathcote and P. J. Allcock; London: Hodder and Stoughton, 1958). The French original appeared in 1955. The material is organized after the manner of Köhler's scheme. For its collection of material and interesting presentation, the book will be valuable to the student; it is not constructed on the grand scale of Eichrodt, von Rad, etc.

Cf. VT 6 (1956) 326–30; RB 64 (1957) 424–27; RSPT

41 (1957) 94–96; RSR 45 (1957) 94–99; *Eleven Years of Bible Bibliography,* p. 753; *Book List* (1959) 29.

226. Köhler, L., *Old Testament Theology* (tr. by A. S. Todd; Philadelphia: Westminster Press, 1957). This work appeared first in 1935; the translation is made from the third German edition (1953), which differs little from the first edition. The material is organized according to the categories borrowed from dogmatic theology: God, man, salvation. The work is deficient in references to the literature, but abounds in word studies.

Cf. JBL 55 (1936) 169–72; RB 45 (1936) 615–17; ZAW 54 (1936) 293–96; RSR 17 (1937) 316–18; TLZ 62 (1937) 30–31; CBQ 19 (1957) 529–30; *Book List* (1958) 35; JSS 4 (1959) 173–75; JBL 78 (1959) 258–59.

227. *McKenzie, J. L., *The Two-edged Sword* (Milwaukee: Bruce, 1956). A survey, with emphasis on the theological content, of the OT books; the material is distributed under such headings as "cosmic origins," "human origins," "king and prophet," "wisdom of the Hebrews," "life and death," etc. It is highly recommended to the general reader for whom it was written.

Cf. CBQ 18 (1956) 422–24; RB 64 (1957) 418; *Interpretation* 11 (1957) 343; *Book List* (1957) 50; Bib 38 (1957) 76–78; JBL 76 (1957) 250–51.

228. Procksch, O., *Theologie des Alten Testaments* (Gütersloh: Bertelsmann, 1950). This is a posthumous work, edited by von Rad. The viewpoint is strongly Christological; the Christian confronts the OT only through Christ. The first part of the work is devoted to the historical background from the patriarchs to the restoration after the Exile;

the second part is systematic and contains the following headings: God and the world; God and people; God and man. References are mainly to much older literature.

Cf. TS 11 (1950) 607–9; 12 (1951) 562–65; RSPT 36 (1952) 147–49; RSR 41 (1953) 471–76; BO 10 (1953) 130–33; Bib 35 (1954) 521–24; *Eleven Years of Bible Bibliography,* pp. 281–82, 358–59.

229. Rad, G. von, *Theologie des Alten Testaments* 1: *Die Theologie der geschichtlichen Überlieferungen Israels* (Munich: Kaiser, 1958). The author is the theologian of Alt's school. In the first main section of this volume, he treats the history of Yahwism and the development of Israel's sacred institutions; the second section is devoted to the problem and method of OT theology, and to a presentation of the "theologies" contained in the Hexateuch, in Judges–Kings, and Chronicles, and finally in the Psalms (Israel's answer to Yahweh). The author rejects the categories of dogmatic theology and any attempt to synthesize in biblical categories; the point of departure is the history of salvation which developed from the cultic proclamation of the kerygma. Even for those who do not share the author's principles, this is an important and stimulating work. A second volume will deal with the prophets.

Cf. TZ 14 (1958) 306–8; ZAW 70 (1958) 271; CBQ 20 (1958) 257–59; RB 65 (1958) 424–27; *Book List* (1958) 37–38; JSS 4 (1959) 286–88; TS 20 (1959) 284–86.

230. Vriezen, Th., *An Outline of Old Testament Theol-*

ogy (tr. by S. Neuijen; Oxford: Blackwell, 1958). The work appeared originally in Dutch (1950); in 1954, a considerably larger second Dutch edition was published and translated into German (1957). For the English translation the second Dutch edition was used, with changes in the bibliography; this translation has a fuller text than the German. The viewpoint of the book differs from that of Eichrodt or von Rad; it intends to be a Christian view of OT theology. After a long introductory section of prolegomena, there follows the theology proper; the material is organized into the headings: God; man; intercourse between God and man; intercourse between man and man; God, man, and the world in the present and future.

Cf. ZAW 62 (1949–50) 312–13; BO 9 (1952) 191–92; 13 (1956) 243; ZAW 68 (1956) 221–22; TZ 13 (1957) 137–38; RB 64 (1957) 132–33; RSPT 42 (1958) 130–32; *Book List* (1958) 40–41; *Interpretation* 13 (1959) 333–36; RB 66 (1959) 132–33; JBL 78 (1959) 256–58; JSS 4 (1959) 393–95; *Eleven Years of Bible Bibliography,* pp. 287, 688.

231. Wright, G. E., *God Who Acts* (London: SCM Press, 1952). The author discusses the problem of method in biblical theology and concludes that the proper method consists in a recital of the great acts of God as developed in the salvation history of the OT and NT. He develops this theme under two heads: what God has done; what man has done. This method has much in common with that of von Rad; there are, however, notable differences in the treatment of the biblical material. This is an

excellent monograph, highly recommended; it appears in the series *Studies in Biblical Theology*.

Cf. RB 60 (1953) 598–600; TLZ 79 (1954) 606–8; JBL 73 (1954) 240–42; RSPT 38 (1954) 104–5; *Eleven Years of Bible Bibliography*, pp. 518–19.

232. Wright, G. E., *The Old Testament against Its Environment* (London: SCM Press, 1950). This little monograph on the nature of Israelite religion, especially as contrasted with the world in which it existed, forms a fine introduction for the author's work on biblical theology. It is highly recommended; it appears in the series *Studies in Biblical Theology*.

Cf. RB 58 (1951) 471–72; JTS n.s. 2 (1951) 186–87; JBL 70 (1951) 321–23; *Eleven Years of Bible Bibliography*, pp. 363–64.

C. NT

233. *Bonsirven, J., *Théologie du Nouveau Testament* (Paris: Aubier, 1951). A sketchy treatment of the theology of the NT, which is not up to the usual level of Bonsirven's writings. It unfortunately treats the Johannine material together with the Synoptics. Four parts: (1) Jesus (His person, message, work); (2) Primitive Community; (3) Paul; (4) Christian Maturity (James, etc.)

Cf. NRT 75 (1953) 426–27; RSPT 36 (1952) 177–78.

234. Bultmann, R., *Theology of the New Testament* (2 vols.; tr. by K. Grobel; London: SCM Press, 1955–56). A subtle, stimulating study of the doctrine of the NT, which is unfortunately based on

certain philosophical presuppositions with which we cannot agree. While the book is *sui generis,* it is nevertheless recommended for discerning readers.

Cf. RB 58 (1951) 252–57; 59 (1952) 93–100; 61 (1954) 432–35; ThR 22 (1954) 21–46; ThZ 11 (1955) 1–27; CQR 157 (1956) 202–4; CBQ 21 (1959) 399–400 (3rd Germ. ed.).

235. Feine, P., *Theologie des Neuen Testaments* (8th ed.; Berlin: Evangelische Verlagsanstalt, 1950). This is an excellent, conservative Protestant theology of the NT, written from the pre-Bultmann standpoint. The numerous editions through which it has gone attest to its abiding value.

Cf. TLZ 60 (1935) 344; 75 (1950) 739; ThRev 22 (1923) 159–60.

236. *Kuss, O., *Die Theologie des Neuen Testaments: Eine Einführung* (2nd ed.; Regensburg: Pustet, 1937). A popular exposé intended for educated laymen.

Cf. NRT 65 (1938) 613–14; ZKT 62 (1938) 281–82.

237. *Meinertz, M., *Theologie des Neuen Testamentes* (Bonnerbibel Ergänzungsband 1–2; Bonn: P. Hanstein, 1950). A thorough and rich coverage of NT theology by a well-known Catholic exegete, which is divided into four parts: (1) Jesus; (2) Primitive Community (Acts, James, Jude); (3) Paul; (4) John. Unfortunately, the OT roots of the NT doctrines are not given quite the adequate treatment that they deserve.

Cf. Bib 32 (1951) 120–26; NRT 74 (1952) 533–34; TS 12 (1951) 112–13; RB 58 (1951) 596–600.

238. Richardson, A., *Introduction to the Theology of the New Testament* (New York: Harper, 1959). This is the latest English attempt to present the theology of the NT in a handy one-volume scope. The author frames a hypothesis concerning the content and character of the faith of the apostolic Church and tests it in the light of all available techniques of NT scholarship. He finds that Jesus Himself is the author of the brilliant reinterpretation of the OT scheme of salvation found in the NT. Though we cannot agree with the author in all points of interpretation, it seems likely that this book will have much influence in the English-speaking world of NT studies, which otherwise lacks such a study.

   Cf. ExpTim 70 (1958–59) 167–68; HJ 57 (1959) 302–4.

239. Stauffer, E., *New Testament Theology* (tr. by J. Marsh; London: SCM Press, 1955). A compact, schematic presentation of the main themes of biblical theology from creation to the Second Coming; rich in bibliography. It is neither in the Bultmann tradition nor does it exaggerate the Hellenistic element in NT thought; it attempts to give due attention to genuine OT traditions and rabbinical material. However, it is filled with highly personal remarks that will not be acceptable to all scholars.

   Cf. ExpTim 67 (1955–56) 8–9; JTS n.s. 7 (1956) 291–93; ATR 38 (1956) 248–51.

⋆ XIII. Biblical Archaeology ⋆

240. Albright, W. F., *Archaeology and the Religion of Israel* (3rd ed.; Baltimore: Johns Hopkins Press, 1953). This work was first published in 1942; in this edition, it is brought up to date by eight closely-printed pages of notes. The archaeological and historical background of premonarchic and monarchic religion in Israel, and of religion at Elephantine. Highly recommended.
   Cf. OLZ 52 (1956) 522–53; ZAW 52 (1957) 352–54; TLZ 83 (1958) 261–64.

241. Albright, W. F., *The Archaeology of Palestine* (5th ed.; Baltimore: Penguin Books, 1960). A slight revision (especially to include the Qumrân scrolls) of the first edition (1949). A survey of archaeological technique and of excavation in Palestine; the organization is by periods (from the Old Stone Age to NT times). The last third of the work is devoted to peoples, languages, writing in Palestine, to daily life in Palestine, and to archaeology and the Old and New Testament. This is an excellent book packed with information.
   Cf. RB 57 (1950) 310–12; *Eleven Years of Bible Bibliography,* p. 230; *Syria* 27 (1950) 152–54; JAOS 70 (1950) 114–15.

242. Albright, W. F., *Recent Discoveries in Bible Lands* (Pittsburgh: Biblical Colloquium, 1955). This

monograph is a reprint of the author's essay in R. Young, *Analytical Concordance to the Bible* (22nd American ed.; New York, 1955). The first half of the book is a survey of the history of excavation in the Near East; the second half relates the archaeological data to the OT and NT. Though comparatively small, the book is filled with information.

Cf. CBQ 18 (1956) 332; TS 17 (1956) 584–85; *Book List* (1957) 15–16; JSS 2 (1957) 396; RB 64 (1957) 419.

243. Barrois, A.-G., *Manuel d'archéologie biblique* (2 vols.; Paris: Picard, 1939, 1953). This handbook of the results of Palestinian archaeology is topically arranged, e.g., ancient towns, fortification, waterworks, farming, family, law, liberal arts. Though Vol. 1 needs revision, this is the best work available. There is an extensive bibliography.

Cf. RB 48 (1939) 603–4; 60 (1953) 596–98; *Syria* 20 (1939) 264–65; 30 (1953) 317–19; Bib 20 (1939) 327–30; 36 (1955) 83–85; ZAW 65 (1953) 82–85; RHR 144 (1953) 222–27; JAOS 74 (1954) 94–96; JBL 74 (1955) 128–30; JNES 14 (1955) 133–35.

244. Burrows, M., *What Mean These Stones?* (New Haven: American Schools of Oriental Research, 1941). A good, interesting survey of the results of archaeology as they illustrate the Bible, and biblical life and institutions.

245. Dalman, G., *Arbeit und Sitte in Palästina* (7 vols.; Gütersloh: Bertelsmann, 1928–42). This is the standard work on life and customs in ancient and modern Palestine. It is unfortunate that the author

did not make much more use of archaeological results.

246. Finegan, J., *Light from the Ancient Past* (2nd ed.; Princeton: Princeton University Press, 1959). This work, first published in 1946, is a very broad survey of the archaeological background from the Judaeo-Christian religion. The author is mainly at the mercy of secondary sources; he has, however, tried to follow the best, and the references to the literature are very full. There are good summaries of the history of Egypt and Mesopotamia, of archaeological work in Palestine, of the late pre-Christian period, of the beginnings of Christianity and its spread in the Roman Empire, and of the sub-apostolic Church. This is a very readable book which will give the beginner an excellent introduction into the background of biblical history. The viewpoint is moderately conservative.

Cf. BA 9 (1946) 43; JNES 5 (1946) 239; JBL 65 (1946) 407–11; Or 17 (1948) 105–8; *Eleven Years of Bible Bibliography*, pp. 69–70; TZ 4 (1948) 346–47.

247. "The Holy Land," *Antiquity and Survival* 2 (1957) 79–317. This issue of the Israeli publication is devoted to archaeological surveys of Palestinian prehistory and to various phases of history and culture in Palestine generally or in particular sites. The work is abundantly illustrated with drawings and plates; there is an archaeologically illustrated table of chronology.

Cf. *Book List* (1958) 12.

248. Kenyon, K., *Beginning in Archaeology* (rev. ed.;

London: Phoenix House, 1953). An excellent introduction to archaeological technique.

Cf. BA 16 (1953) 43–44; CBQ 15 (1953) 264; *Eleven Years of Bible Bibliography,* p. 472.

249. McCown, C. C., *The Ladder of Progress in Palestine* (New York: Harper, 1943). Description, with wealth of detail, of the rediscovery of Palestine through excavation; the archaeological data are organized historically from the Old Stone Age to the Crusades, though a few sites, e.g., Tell Beit Mirsim, Beth-Shan, Samaria, are treated in distinct chapters. In the nearly twenty years since this book appeared, much more has been added to our knowledge, but for the period covered this book is very worth while. There is a relatively large bibliography, especially of the excavation reports.

250. Parrot, A. (ed.), *Cahiers d'archéologie biblique* (Neuchâtel: Delachaux et Niestlé, 1952—). These monographs, now numbering ten, treat of specific subjects on which contemporary archaeology throws light; there is an introductory volume (unnumbered) which gives a general survey of Near Eastern archaeology. Parrot himself has written eight of the volumes. Many of them have been translated into English. So far, the following have appeared: *Découverte des mondes ensevelis; Déluge et arche de Noé* (1); *La tour de Babel* (2); *Ninivé et l'Ancien Testament* (3); *Les routes de saint Paul dans l'Orient grec* (4); *Le temple de Jérusalem* (5); *Golgotha et Saint-Sépulcre* (6); *Samarie, capitale du royaume d'Israël* (7); *Baby-*

lone et l'Ancien Testament (8); *Le Musée du Louvre et la Bible* (9); *Sur la pierre et l'argile* (10). These volumes have been very well received and can be warmly recommended.

251. Pritchard, J., *Archaeology and the Old Testament* (Princeton: Princeton University Press, 1958). A useful book surveying the materials of archaeology, the techniques of topography, and the story of the excavations and their contributions in Mesopotamia and at Ras Shamra.
Cf. JSS 4 (1959) 278–79.

252. *Vaux, R. de, *Les institutions de l'Ancien Testament* (2 vols.; Paris: Ed. du Cerf). A supplementary volume of the Jerusalem Bible. Vol. 1 (1958) is devoted to nomadism and its survivals in Israel, to family institutions (marriage, inheritance, burials, children, etc.), and to civil institutions (kingship, idea of the state, slavery, calendar, etc.); Vol. 2 (1960) covers military and religious institutions. Though meant for the nonspecialist, this work is the product of the author's profound scholarship and balanced judgment. It is an indispensable handbook for biblical study.
Cf. *Book List* (1958) 39; VT 8 (1958) 321–26; TS 19 (1958) 415–16; CBQ 20 (1958) 556–57; JSS 4 (1959) 169–71.

253. Wheeler, R. E. M., *Archaeology from the Earth* (Oxford: Clarendon Press, 1954). A fuller explanation of archaeological technique than in Kenyon's volume. Though the book is not concerned expressly with biblical archaeology, and though many

examples are drawn from far outside the biblical field, it can be highly recommended to the biblical student.

254. Wiseman, D. J., *Illustrations from Biblical Archaeology* (London: Tyndale Press, 1958). Over one hundred pictures, of which a few are published for the first time, to illustrate the OT and NT; there is an explanatory text. In spite of mistakes in the book, the student will profit from the collection.

255. Wright, G. E., *Biblical Archaeology* (Philadelphia: Westminster Press, 1957). This is a comprehensive survey of all the archaeological information available which illuminates the OT and NT; the material is arranged in historical sequence from prehistoric times to the NT period. This is an excellent work, which will be used most profitably with the *Westminster Atlas*.

Cf. CBQ 19 (1957) 528–29; JSS 2 (1957) 392–93; AJA 62 (1958) 112–13; RB 65 (1958) 312; JBL 77 (1958) 78–80; ZAW 70 (1958) 167–70; TLZ 84 (1959) 94–98; *Interpretation* 13 (1959) 107–9.

★ XIV. Biblical Geography ★

256. *Abel, F.-M., *Géographie de la Palestine* (2 vols.; Paris: Gabalda, 1933, 1938). Though in need of revision, these volumes remain the standard reference work on Palestinian geography. Vol. 1 is devoted to physical and historical geography; Vol. 2 covers political geography and gives an extensive list of biblical and other historical sites with references to ancient sources and modern discussions.

Cf. JPOS 15 (1935) 185–90; JBL 58 (1939) 177–87.

257. *Baldi, D., *Enchiridion locorum sanctorum: Documenta s. Evangelii loca respicientia* (2nd ed.; Jerusalem: Typis PP. Franciscanorum, 1955). Ancient descriptions of NT sites, preserved in the NT itself, patristic writers, medieval and Renaissance pilgrims and travelers, have been collected in this handy volume. The original text is usually given together with a Latin translation below it on the same page. Very useful.

Cf. Bib 37 (1956) 93–94; RB 63 (1956) 157–58; see also RB 45 (1936) 158–59 (1st ed.).

258. Baly, D., *The Geography of the Bible* (New York: Harper, 1957). This is not a historical geography; organization follows properly geographical lines. The first part treats of geology, soil, climate, fauna, flora, etc.; in Part 2, each of the five main divisions

of Palestine is described with special emphasis on the geological structure. This is a valuable book, packed with information, though at times the beginner may find himself lost in details.

Cf. JBR 25 (1957) 364–65; JBL 76 (1957) 333–35; *Interpretation* 12 (1958) 88–91; *Book List* (1958) 14; JSS 4 (1959) 63–64.

259. *Buit, M. du, *Géographie de la Terre sainte* (2 vols.; Paris: Ed. du Cerf, 1958). This work is part of the supplementary volumes of the Jerusalem Bible. Vol. 1 covers the physical and historical geography and gives a topographical index with biblical references and brief notes; Vol. 2 is a collection of eighteen maps. Very useful for the biblical student.

Cf. CBQ 21 (1959) 385–87; *Book List* (1959) 12; JBL 78 (1959) 265–66; RB 66 (1959) 305–6.

260. *Grollenberg, L. H., *Atlas of the Bible* (tr. and ed. by J. M. H. Reid and H. H. Rowley; London: Nelson, 1956). This is a historical geography which appeared first in Dutch and later in French; the translation has been made from the latter. Perhaps the most important feature of this work is the collection of over four hundred illustrative pictures; each is adequately identified. By an ingenious use of symbols, a great deal of information is incorporated on the maps. The text, however, is in many ways inferior to that of the *Westminster Atlas*. The book is up-to-date and scientific; it is highly recommended.

Cf. RB 62 (1955) 595–97; Bib 37 (1956) 84–87; JSS 1 (1956) 83; 2 (1957) 281–82; CBQ 19 (1957) 270–71; *Eleven Years of Bible Bibliography*, p. 654.

261. *Lemaire, P., and Baldi, D., *Atlante storico della Bibbia* (Turin: Marietti, 1955). A supplementary volume of *La sacra Bibbia*. This is a very useful work of commendable scholarship, though it will not replace either Grollenberg's atlas or the *Westminster Atlas*.

Cf. RB 63 (1956) 423–27; Bib 37 (1956) 81–84; *Eleven Years of Bible Bibliography*, p. 725.

262. Smith, G. A., *Historical Geography of the Holy Land* (4th ed.; London: Hodder and Stoughton, 1896). First published in 1894; the many "editions" since 1896 are just reprints of the fourth. Though now outmoded in much of its detail, this work still remains classic. In 1915, Smith published an accompanying atlas which, too, is now out-of-date.

263. Wright, G. E., and Filson, F. V., *The Westminster Historical Atlas to the Bible* (rev. ed.; Philadelphia: Westminster Press, 1956). The text of this work has undergone considerable revision in detail, and new sections have been added on the rise of Jewish sects and on archaeological progress in Palestine; some new pictures have been introduced, while others have been dropped; new identifications have been incorporated on the maps. The text is probably the best of the recent historical geographies.

Cf. Bib 38 (1957) 357–58; CBQ 19 (1957) 390; TLZ 82 (1957) 496–99; JBL 76 (1957) 256–57; JSS 2 (1957) 283–84.

★ XV. History ★

264. *Abel, F.-M., *Histoire de la Palestine* (2 vols.; Paris: Gabalda, 1952). Vol. 1 covers the political history of Palestine from the conquest of Alexander to the first Jewish revolt; Vol. 2 continues the history to the Arab conquest. This is a remarkable synthesis of a thousand years of history by a deep and balanced scholar. Though not all his views will be accepted by scholars, and though progress in historical knowledge may modify many which are admitted, this work is fundamental for the background of late pre-Christian Judaism and for Christian times.

Cf. *Eleven Years of Bible Bibliography,* p. 392; RB 60 (1953) 631–32; JBL 73 (1954) 108–9; Bib 35 (1954) 246–49; OLZ 49 (1954) 43–46.

265. Albright, W. F., *From the Stone Age to Christianity* (2nd ed. with new introduction; Garden City, N.Y.: Doubleday Anchor Books, 1957). This monumental work of theologico-historical synthesis first appeared in 1940 and was revised in 1946; the new introduction provides the author's latest positions.

Cf. RB 54 (1947) 435–40; TZ 4 (1948) 348–53; ZAW 61 (1945–48) 239–43; Bib 32 (1951) 305–11; 39 (1958) 361–62; Or 20 (1951) 216–36; JSS 2 (1957) 427–28; CBQ 20 (1958) 109–10.

266. Albright, W. F., *The Biblical Period* (Pittsburgh:

Biblical Colloquium, 1950). This booklet is a reprint of L. Finkelstein, *The Jews* 1, chap 1. In broad outlines, it traces the history of Israel from the Mosaic period to the restoration. This little work is packed with information.

267. Bright, J., *Early History in Recent History Writing* (London: SCM Press, 1956). An excellent exposition and critique of the historical methods of the Alt-Noth school; there is a briefer summary of the work of Y. Kaufmann. The author finally draws up an outline of the method to be followed in writing the early history of Israel. A knowledge of this book is requisite for an understanding of Bright's own history of Israel.

Cf. *Book List* (1957) 23; JBL 76 (1957) 249; *Interpretation* 11 (1957) 461–63; CBQ 19 (1957) 392–96; JSS 4 (1959) 72–73.

268. Bright, J., *A History of Israel* (Philadelphia: Westminster Press, 1959). This is the first systematic history from Albright's school. In spite of some weaknesses, this book is highly recommended.

269. Foerster, W., *Neutestamentliche Zeitgeschichte* (Die urchristliche Botschaft 26; Hamburg: Furche-Verlag, Part 1 [Das Judentum Palästinas zur Zeit Jesu und der Apostel, 1955]; Part 2 [Das römische Weltreich zur Zeit des Neuen Testaments, 1956]). Vol. 1 first appeared during the difficult time of the war, 1940; the 1955 issue is a revised edition. This is probably the best up-to-date history of NT times that we have at present; the two slender volumes

even take into account the data from the Dead Sea Scrolls.

Cf. JBL 75 (1956) 58–59; 76 (1957) 62–64; TQ 137 (1957) 87–88.

270. Jackson, F. J. F., and Lake, K. (edd.), *The Beginnings of Christianity* (London: Macmillan, Part 1: The Acts of the Apostles, Vol. 1 [1939], 2 [1922], 3 [1926], 4 [1933], 5 [1933]). This is actually a monumental commentary on the book of the Acts of the Apostles, but it contains many invaluable excursus on the history of the times of the early Church. Only Part 1 has appeared.

Cf. JTS 34 (1933) 271–75; RB 30 (1921) 453–59; 42 (1933) 423–27.

271. Jones, A. H. M., *The Cities of the Eastern Roman Provinces* (Oxford: Clarendon Press, 1937). The author's purpose is "to trace the diffusion of the Greek city as a political institution through the lands bordering on the eastern Mediterranean which were included within the Roman empire." It deals mainly with the period after Alexander in the time of the Hellenistic kings; it tries to show the effect that incorporation into Roman provinces had on the cities of that area. A very useful book for the understanding of the Hellenization of the world in which the NT grew up.

Cf. JPOS 18 (1938) 139–40.

272. Kittel, R., *Geschichte des Volkes Israel* (3 vols.; Stuttgart: W. Kohlhammer, Vol. 1 [6th ed.], 1923; Vol. 2 [6th ed.], 1925; Vol. 3, 1927–29). In its time

this work was classic, and it may still be consulted with profit.

273. Magie, D., *Roman Rule in Asia Minor, to the End of the Third Century after Christ* (2 vols.; Princeton: Princeton University Press, 1950). The author's purpose is "to present what is known of the expansion of Rome's Empire in Asia Minor and the lands adjacent on the east and of her rule over the Asianic provinces . . . to the end of the third century after Christ." Vol. 1 contains the text of Magie's study, Vol. 2 his abundant notes. An excellent background for the study of the cities mentioned in Acts and the Pauline letters.

    Cf. CHR 38 (1952–53) 342–43; CP 48 (1952) 235–38.

274. Noth, M., *Geschichte Israels* (2nd ed.; Göttingen: Vandenhoeck & Ruprecht, 1954). Apart from minor changes in the text, additional references to literature, expansion of the bibliography, and an index of biblical passages, this edition does not differ from the first (1950). Except for the treatment of Israel's early history, this work is highly recommended.

    Cf. *Eleven Years of Bible Bibliography,* pp. 321–22; RB 58 (1951) 474–76; 62 (1955) 280–81; TLZ 76 (1951) 335–40; 77 (1952) 677–84; VT 1 (1951) 72–74; JBL 73 (1954) 106–8; JSS 4 (1959) 151–64; J. Bright, *Early Israel in Recent Historical Writing.*

275. Noth, M., *The History of Israel* (new tr. by G. B. F. Brandon; New York: Harper, 1959). This new, corrected translation now replaces the defective original translation (1958); the first translation cannot be safely used.

276. Oesterley, W. O. E., and Robinson, T. H., *A History of Israel* (2 vols.; Oxford: Clarendon Press, 1932). For a long time this was the standard history of Israel for English readers. With due caution, parts of it can still be used.
Cf. JPOS 12 (1932) 251–67.

277. Rostovtzeff, M. I., *The Social and Economic History of the Hellenistic World* (3 vols.; Oxford: Clarendon Press, 1941). A study of the period from Alexander to Augustus, especially of the world created by Alexander's conquest of the East and of the states into which it disintegrated as long as they retained political independence and the Greeks in those states held the leading role in all spheres of life.

278. Schürer, E., *Geschichte des jüdischen Volkes im Zeitalter Jesu Christi* (4th ed.; Leipzig: Hinrichs, 1901–11). Though this work is old, it is still quite useful, as there are many aspects of Jewish history in the time of Christ that are treated here and have not found better treatment since then. An English translation, prepared by J. MacPherson *et al.,* was based on the second German edition: *A History of the Jewish People in the Time of Jesus Christ* (Edinburgh: T. and T. Clark, Division 1, Vol. 1 [1905], Vol. 2 [1905]; Division 2, Vol. 1 [1901], Vol. 2 [1901], Vol. 3 [n. d.]; Index [1898]).

278a. Tcherikover, V., *Hellenistic Civilization and the Jews* (tr. by S. Applebaum; Philadelphia: Jewish Publication Society of America, 1959). This work of the professor of classical history in the Hebrew

University appears posthumously. It provides good scholarly background for the history and culture of the Jews between the conquest of Alexander and the Roman period.

* XVI. Intertestamental Period *

A. Texts

279. Charles, R. H. (ed.), *The Apocrypha and Pseudepigrapha of the Old Testament* (2 vols.; Oxford: Clarendon Press, 1913). This work contains translations, done by various scholars, of the apocryphal (deuterocanonical) and pseudepigraphical (apocryphal) works of the OT; there are also extensive introductions, critical and explanatory notes, and topical indices. Though this must remain the current reference work for these texts, a great deal of revision is needed.

280. Kautzsch, E. (ed.), *Die Apokryphen und Pseudepigraphen des Alten Testaments* (2 vols.; Tübingen: J. C. B. Mohr, 1900). Translations and brief notes of almost the same materials found in Charles's edition. Also very much in need of revision.

281. *Riessler, P., *Altjüdisches Schrifttum ausserhalb der Bibel übersetzt und erläutert* (Augsburg: B. Filser, 1928). The collection of nonbiblical Jewish texts here translated is much more extensive than that of Charles's edition. Since it brings together many texts which are ordinarily difficult to find, the book is useful; it should not be used for scholarly work.
Cf. Bib 9 (1928) 473–76.

282. Zeitlin, S. (ed.), *Jewish Apocryphal Literature* (New York: Harper, 1950—). This series, sponsored by the Dropsie College, is planned as a new edition of the Apocrypha (deuterocanonical books) and pseudepigrapha. Original texts and translations are given, and there are extensive introductions and comments; some volumes discuss particular questions in appendices. This is a very useful series.

B. Studies

283. Bousset, W., *Die Religion des Judentums im späthellenistischen Zeitalter* (3rd. improved ed. by H. Gressmann; Tübingen: J. C. B. Mohr, 1926). This monumental work on pre-Christian Jewish religion contains a long introduction (pp. 6–52) surveying the sources; these latter, of course, include the apocryphal and pseudepigraphical works.

284. *Lagrange, M.-J., *Judaïsme avant Jésus-Christ* (2nd ed.; Paris: Gabalda, 1931). An excellent historical, doctrinal, and literary survey of Judaism in the pre-Christian period. It would now need considerable revision in details.

Cf. also the entries under *Introductions to the Bible* and *Commentaries in Series*.

★ XVII. The Dead Sea Scrolls ★

A. Primary Texts

285. Avigad, N., and Yadin, Y., *A Genesis Apocryphon,
a Scroll from the Wilderness of Judaea, Description
and Contents of the Scroll, Facsimiles, Transcription and Translation of Columns II, XIX–XXII*
(Jerusalem: Magnes Press of the Hebrew University, 1956). This is a preliminary publication of
the seventh scroll of Qumrân Cave 1, issued to give
scholars access to part of it while the rest of the
scroll which required very delicate treatment for
opening was being tediously worked on. The translation and introduction are written in both English
and modern Hebrew.

    Cf. Bib 38 (1957) 461; JNES 18 (1959) 82–84; OLZ
53 (1958) 453–54; TLZ 82 (1957) 257–62.

286. *Barthélemy, D., and Milik, J. T., *Qumran Cave 1*
(Discoveries in the Judaean Desert 1; Oxford:
Clarendon Press, 1955). This volume contains the
official archaeological report of the excavation of
Cave 1, contributed by R. de Vaux, G. M. Crow-
foot, H. J. Plenderleith, and G. L. Harding. But the
main contribution is the publication of the fragments of some seventy different scrolls that had also
been hidden in Cave 1 along with the seven major
ones. This volume is the first in the series, of which
about a dozen are projected, for the full publication

of the fragments from Qumrân Caves 2–11, from the caves of the Wâdi Murabba'ât, and from the site of Khirbet Mird.

Cf. Bib 37 (1956) 231–35; CBQ 18 (1956) 77–79; RB 63 (1956) 110–14; ZAW 67 (1955) 131–39.

287. Burrows, M. (ed.), *The Dead Sea Scrolls of St. Mark's Monastery* (New Haven: American Schools of Oriental Research). Vol. 1, containing the photographs and transcription of the Isaiah Manuscript (1QIs^a) and of the Habakkuk Commentary (1QpHab), was published in 1950; a corrected reprint (with considerably poorer photographs) appeared in 1953. Vol. 2, fasc. 2, containing the plates and transcription of the Manual of Discipline (1QS), appeared in 1951. Fasc. 1 of Vol. 2, which was to be devoted to the fourth scroll of Cave 1 (called today the "Genesis Apocryphon"), never appeared.

Cf. ZAW 64 (1952) 68; Bib 34 (1953) 403–4; MUSJ 29 (1951–52) 375 ff.

288. Sukenik, E. L., *The Dead Sea Scrolls of the Hebrew University* (Jerusalem: Magnes Press of the Hebrew University, 1955). First published under the Hebrew title, *'Ôṣar hamm^egillôt hagg^enûzôt* (Jerusalem: Bialik Foundation and the Hebrew University, 1954). This publication presents the photographs and transcription of the remaining three great scrolls of Cave 1: Isaiah B (1QIs^b), the War Scroll (1QM), and the Thanksgiving Psalms or *Hôdāyôt* (1QH).

Cf. Bib 37 (1956) 227–30; RB 62 (1955) 597–601; JBL 75 (1956) 87–88.

B. Tools and Secondary Studies

289. Burchard, C., *Bibliographie zu den Handschriften vom Toten Meer* (Beiheft zur ZAW 76; Berlin: A. Töpelmann, 1957). An almost exhaustive bibliography of serious writings covering the period from 1949 to 1956, containing 1538 entries listed alphabetically according to the names of the authors. Book reviews are included. This bibliography is being continued in the *Revue de Qumran* (see §299); first supplement appeared in RQ 1 (1958–59) 461–79. It is indispensable for the study of the Scrolls.

   Cf. Bib 38 (1957) 461; HJ 56 (1957–58) 192–94.

290. Burrows, M., *The Dead Sea Scrolls, with Translations by the Author* (New York: Viking, 1955). An excellent introduction to the study of the Scrolls, written by a scholar who was identified with the question from its very beginning.

   Cf. CBQ 18 (1956) 188–91; RB 63 (1956) 471–72; Bib 37 (1956) 514–15.

291. Burrows, M., *More Light on the Dead Sea Scrolls, New Scrolls and New Interpretations, with Translations of Important Recent Discoveries* (New York: Viking, 1958). This is Burrows' "second phase" book on the Scrolls. Together with the former book, it affords an excellent introduction to the subject for anyone who wishes to begin a serious study. Abundant bibliographies are found in both books, which are devoid of the scientific apparatus of footnotes. Almost one hundred pages are given over to the discussion of "Christian

Origins in the Light of the Dead Sea Scrolls." For a complete view of the problems raised by the Scrolls, this and the former book by Burrows cannot be recommended too highly.

Cf. NTA 3 (1958) 117.

292. Cross, F. M., Jr., *The Ancient Library of Qumran and Modern Biblical Studies* (New York: Doubleday, 1958). This book, which is one of the two best on the Scrolls today, grew out of the Haskell Lectures 1956–57, delivered to the Graduate School of Theology at Oberlin College. It presents an interesting account of the discovery of the ancient library, of the Essenes, the people of the Scrolls, of the Righteous Teacher, their founder, and of the importance of the Qumrân Scrolls for OT study and for the study of the primitive Church. Like Milik's book, it too presupposes an elementary knowledge of the Scrolls.

Cf. RQ 3 (1959) 440–43; JBL 78 (1959) 78–80; Bib 39 (1958) 511–15.

293. Kuhn, K. G., *Konkordanz zu den Qumrantexten* (Göttingen: Vandenhoeck & Ruprecht, 1960). The work includes all the nonbiblical Hebrew texts from Qumrân and the Damascus Document from Cairo published so far. A supplement will follow for texts to be published later.

294. Kuhn, K. G. (ed.), *Dictionary of the Qumran Texts* (Göttingen: Vandenhoeck & Ruprecht, 196?). Announced for publication soon. Though the title of this work is given in English, the sample pages advertised show that it will be a German

work. It intends to present the usages of nonbiblical Hebrew of the Qumrân texts, together with references to literature (discussions) of the words in question.

295. LaSor, W. S., "Bibliography of the Dead Sea Scrolls 1948–1957," *Fuller Library Bulletin* 31 (Fall 1958) [= Fuller Theological Seminary Bibliographical Series 2; Pasadena, Cal.: Fuller Theological Seminary, 1958]. Another bibliography of the Dead Sea Scrolls, which differs from that of Burchard in that the entries are arranged by subjects (with abundant cross references). It is for this reason often more useful than Burchard's.

Cf. CBQ 22 (1960) 118.

296. *Milik, J. T., *Ten Years of Discovery in the Wilderness of Judaea* (Studies in Biblical Theology 26; Naperville, Ill.: A. R. Allenson, 1959). One of the two best books on the Scrolls, which attempts to present a learned synthesis of all the data that has emerged from the study of them during the last ten years. Though a fascinating, readable account, it presupposes an elementary knowledge about the Scrolls and their contents. This English edition was prepared by J. Strugnell and represents a complete reworking of the material of the French edition, *Dix ans de découvertes dans le désert de Juda* (Paris: Ed. du Cerf, 1957).

Cf. RB 64 (1957) 633–36; CBQ 19 (1957) 358–59; 21 (1959) 96–99; TS 20 (1959) 448–51.

297. *Nötscher, F., *Zur theologischen Terminologie der Qumrantexte* (Bonner biblische Beiträge 10; Bonn:

P. Hanstein, 1956). An attempt at a systematic presentation of the theological notions of gnosis, dualism, light and darkness, eschatology, eternity and retribution, as found in the Qumrân texts that have been published so far. This is an early attempt to codify the Essenes' theology, which is laudable but sketchy. It is, however, quite useful and will remain so until further, more thorough studies are undertaken.

Cf. CBQ 19 (1957) 134; BZ 1 (1957) 157–58; ETL 32 (1956) 379–80.

298. *Ploeg, J. van der, *The Excavations at Qumran: A Survey of the Judaean Brotherhood and Its Ideas* (tr. by K. Smyth; London: Longmans, Green, 1958). A handy one-volume survey of the initial finds and their significance; a good short book to start with. It was translated from the Dutch, *Vondsten in de woestijn van Juda: De rollen van der Dode Zee* (Prisma Boeken; Utrecht: Spectrum, 1957).

Cf. RB 64 (1957) 630–31; JSS 2 (1957) 412–13.

299. *Revue de Qumran.* A periodical devoted to studies of the Dead Sea Scrolls, begun in 1958 by M. l'Abbé J. Carmignac, published by Letouzey et Ané, Paris. Contributions are written in English, French, German, Italian, Latin, and Spanish. Its aim is to have scholars who write on the Scrolls publish in one centralized organ, but it is not likely that it will deter them from publishing elsewhere as well.

300. Stendahl, K. (ed.), *The Scrolls and the New Testament* (New York: Harper, 1957). A collection of

fourteen essays by twelve NT scholars on the relation of the Scrolls to the NT. They are technical discussions and are not intended for the general reader.

Cf. RB 66 (1959) 152–55; summary of reviews, NTA 3 (1959) 315–18.

301. *Vermès, G., *Discovery in the Judean Desert* (New York: Desclée, 1956). An English translation of the French second edition of *Les manuscrits du désert de Juda,* which was one of the best European surveys of the first phase of the discovery and work on the Scrolls.

Cf. JBL 75 (1956) 157–59; JSS 1 (1956) 184–85; RB 61 (1954) 630–31.

* XVIII. New Testament Apocrypha *

302. *Amiot, F., *La Bible apocryphe: Evangiles apocryphes* (Textes pour l'histoire sacrée; Paris: Fayard, 1952). Despite its title, this little book contains French translations not only of the apocryphal Gospels, but also of some of the Agrapha, the apocryphal Acts, Epistles, and Apocalypses. It is a handy collection of select translations in a small paper-back.

    Cf. Bib 35 (1954) 107.

303. Hennecke, E., *Neutestamentliche Apokryphen in deutscher Übersetzung* (3rd fully rev. ed. by W. Schneemelcher; Tübingen: J. C. B. Mohr, Vol. 1 [1959], Vol. 2 [announced]). First published in 1904 under the title *Handbuch zu den neutestamentlichen Apokryphen,* the second edition appeared in 1924 with the present title. This work has long been regarded as the basic text of the NT Apocrypha in a modern translation. Important bibliographical material is indicated for each of the writings. The new edition contains large sections devoted to the Gnostic texts of Chenoboskion.

    Cf. JTS 25 (1923–24) 184–89, 422–25; RHPR 4 (1924) 485–88; RHE 20 (1924) 580–82; TS 21 (1960) 292–94.

304. James, M. R., *The Apocryphal New Testament:*

Being the Apocryphal Gospels, Acts, Epistles and Apocalypses (Oxford: Clarendon Press, 1953). An excellent one-volume collection of English translations of the most important NT Apocrypha, first published in 1924.

Cf. JTS 26 (1924–25) 181–85.

305. Michaelis, W., *Die apokryphen Schriften zum Neuen Testament* (Sammlung Dieterich 129; Bremen: Schünemann, 1956). A handy collection of NT Apocrypha for the general reader, gathered, translated, and commented on by a well-known NT scholar.

Cf. Schol 32 (1957) 619–20; BenMon 33 (1957) 325–26.

★ XIX. Rabbinical Literature ★
(Pertaining to the NT)

A. Texts

306. *Bonsirven, J., *Textes rabbiniques des deux premiers siècles chrétiens pour servir à l'intelligence du Nouveau Testament* (Rome: Pontificio Istituto Biblico, 1955). A collection of texts excerpted from the *Pirqe Aboth,* the *Tannaitic Midrashim,* the *Mishnah,* the *Talmuds,* and the *Tosephta,* arranged not according to the passages of the NT (like Strack-Billerbeck) but according to the rabbinical tractates themselves. Useful indices facilitate the study of themes, the OT passages cited, and the NT passages which the texts illustrate. A useful collection.

Cf. CBQ 17 (1955) 664; RB 63 (1956) 153–54; NTS 2 (1955–56) 209–12.

307. Danby, H., *The Mishnah, Translated from the Hebrew with Introduction and Brief Explanatory Notes* (Oxford: Clarendon Press, 1933; reprinted 1954). This is the standard English translation of the whole Mishnah. Very useful.

Cf. PEFQS 67 (1935) 49–52; JTS 35 (1934) 332–33.

308. Epstein, I. (ed.), *The Babylonian Talmud* (35 vols.; London: Soncino Press, 1935–52). A modern translation of the complete Babylonian Talmud.

Cf. RSR 26 (1936) 229–30.

309. Freedman, H., and Simon, M. (edd.), *Midrash Rabbah* (9 vols.; London–Bournemouth: Soncino Press, 1951). The first eight volumes contain a modern English translation of the Great Midrash on Genesis (two volumes), Exodus, Leviticus, Numbers (two volumes), Deuteronomy and Lamentations, Ruth and Ecclesiastes. Vol. 9 contains a useful glossary, general index, and scriptural references.

310. Kittel, G., and Rengstorf, K. H. (edd.), *Rabbinische Texte* (Stuttgart: W. Kohlhammer). There are two important series in this collection: *Erste Reihe* contains *Die Tosefta* with the text, translation into German, and explanations; *Zweite Reihe* contains the *Tannaitische Midraschim* in translation and explanation. The collection was begun in 1930 but was interrupted in Nazi times and has recently been resurrected.
    Cf. JTS 34 (1933) 421–22.

311. *Die Mischna: Text, Übersetzung und ausführliche Erklärung* (Berlin: A. Töpelmann, 1912–). Interrupted by the two wars, this series of individual commentaries on all the tractates of the Mishnah, giving a vocalized Hebrew text, German translation, and commentary, is most useful.

B. Studies

312. *Bonsirven, J., *Le Judaïsme palestinien aux temps de Jésus-Christ: Sa théologie* (2 vols.; Bibliothèque de théologie historique; 2nd ed.; Paris: Beauchesne,

1934–35). This is a study of Tannaitic Judaism of Palestine in the time of Christ and is based on the rabbinical writings (mainly the Talmudim and Midrashim) critically used, as well as the NT itself, the pseudepigrapha of the OT, Philo, and Josephus. It contains two parts: (1) La théologie dogmatique; (2) Théologie morale, vie morale et religieuse. Many reviewers have praised the "many-sided excellence of this work" (Thomas).

Cf. NRT 63 (1936) 83–86; JTS 37 (1936) 85–87; RB 45 (1936) 263–65.

313. Moore, G. F., *Judaism in the First Centuries of the Christian Era: The Age of the Tannaim* (3 vols.: Cambridge, Mass.: Harvard University Press, 1927–30). A critical evaluation of the Judaism of Palestine in the first centuries of the Christian era by a Gentile scholar who is a recognized authority in the field. An excellent work that has not been surpassed.

Cf. ExpTim 39 (1927–28) 374–78.

314. Strack, H. L., *Introduction to the Talmud and Midrash* (Philadelphia: Jewish Publication Society of America, 1931). An English translation of the Author's Revised Copy of the fifth German edition. It provides a good beginning for one wishing to initiate himself into the mysteries of rabbinical literature.

Cf. ZKT 45 (1921) 293–97; JTS 23 (1921) 200–203.

315. Strack, H. L., and Billerbeck, P., *Kommentar zum Neuen Testament aus Talmud und Midrasch* (5 vols.; Munich: C. H. Beck, 1922, 1924, 1926, 1928,

1956). This is an indispensable tool for the study of the NT, since it gives abundant citations from the rabbinical writings to illustrate many of the passages of the NT. These writings are for the most part later than the NT, but they often incorporate material which is judged contemporary with it. Discrimination is needed to use this work correctly and with profit. Vol. 4 (in two parts) contains some invaluable *Exkurse*.

Cf. ZNW 22 (1923) 156–57; ZKT 47 (1923) 577–80.

⋆ XX. Miscellany ⋆

316. Barrett, C. K., *The New Testament Background: Selected Documents* (London: SPCK, 1956; reprinted 1958). A compilation of over two hundred documents in translation (most of them from Latin and Greek sources) to illustrate the most significant aspects of the civilized world in which Christianity was born. The texts come from the historians, papyri, inscriptions, philosophers, mystery religions, Jewish history, rabbinical literature, Philo, Josephus, the LXX, apocalyptic literature, and Essene writings.

   Cf. summary of reviews in NTA 2 (1957) 91.

317. Deissmann, A., *Light from the Ancient East: The New Testament Illustrated by Recently Discovered Texts of the Graeco-Roman World* (tr. by L. R. M. Strachan; London: Hodder and Stoughton, 1910). Though old, this book is still of very great utility, for it attempts to show how the discoveries of Greek texts in the Egyptian papyri have shed abundant light on the language of the NT.

   Cf. JTS 11 (1909–10) 129–31; 12 (1910–11) 148–49.

318. Dhorme, P. (E.), *Langues et écritures sémitiques* (Paris: Geuthner, 1930). Though this work is old, it will give the student a good idea of the corpus of ancient Semitic literature, and particularly of the collections and journals in which it is published.

319. Fleisch, H., *Introduction à l'étude des langues sémitiques* (Paris: Adrien-Maisonneuve, 1947). Brief description of the Semitic languages, ancient and modern, and critical evaluation of the tools for studying them. The work needs considerable revision to include many new publications and editions. The student can gain a fairly good idea of the "instruments de travail" which appeared before 1947.

320. Galling, K. (ed.), *Textbuch zur Geschichte Israels* (Tübingen: J. C. B. Mohr, 1950). A collection of fifty-seven texts extending down into the first Christian centuries. The Egyptian and Accadian texts are translated; the rest are printed in the original Hebrew, Aramaic, and Greek, and supplied with notes. Useful, especially for the later texts.

Cf. JBL 70 (1950) 164; RB 58 (1951) 273–74; TZ 7 (1950) 131–33.

321. Grant, F. C., *Hellenistic Religions: The Age of Syncretism* (Library of Religion 2; New York: Liberal Arts Press, 1953). This is a collection of texts in translation, offering readings in four aspects of ancient syncretism: (1) Institutional Religion; (2) Criticism of Traditional Religion; (3) Major Cults (Orphic, Oriental, Egyptian, Attis, and Mithras); (4) Religious Ideas of the Philosophers (Epictetus, Epicurus, Plotinus, Proclus, Iamblichus, and Sallustius). The collection is quite handy and useful, but one will not always agree with the interpretations of the editor.

Cf. JR 35 (1955) 125–26; JNES 14 (1955) 195–96; CBQ 16 (1954) 501–2.

322. Grant, F. C. (ed.), *Ancient Roman Religion* (Library of Religion 8; New York: Liberal Arts Press, 1957). A collection of texts from ancient Latin writers and inscriptions, which illustrate various phases of Roman religion: (1) Old Agricultural Religion; (2) Foreign Influences; (3) Philosophy and Religion; (4) Religion under the Imperial Republic; (5) The Augustan Restoration; (6) Religion under the Empire; (7) The Christian Victory and the Pagan Reaction.
Cf. CBQ 20 (1958) 130–32.

AOT 323. Gressmann, H. (ed.), *Altorientalische Texte und*
AOB *Bilder zum Alten Testament* (2nd ed.; Berlin: W. de Gruyter, 1926–27). The first volume presents translations of numerous nonbiblical texts, grouped according to language, which serve to illustrate the Bible; the second volume is a large collection of pictures to illustrate the same. The English reader can now use the more recent work edited by J. Pritchard (see below).

324. Mendelsohn, I. (ed.), *Religions of the Ancient Near East: Sumero-Akkadian Religious Texts and Ugaritic Epics* (New York: Liberal Arts Press, 1955). This is a reprint of materials from ANET, selected to illustrate the religions of the Near East. Mendelsohn has added translations of Shurpu and Maqlu texts which are not included in ANET.

325. Noth, M., *Die Welt des Alten Testaments* (3rd ed.; Berlin: A. Töpelmann, 1957). This work, originally published in 1940, appeared in a considerably revised and augmented second edition in 1952; the third edition is a reprint of the second with six

pages of additional references to more recent literature. In compact form, the book contains a mass of
reliable information on Palestinian geography and
archaeology, on non-Israelite peoples, cultures, languages, etc., and on the text and versions of the
OT. It is an extremely valuable introduction to the
background of the Bible.

Cf. RB 60 (1953) 430–31; BA 16 (1953) 44; TLZ 81
(1956) 155; ArOr 22 (1954) 485–86; BO 11 (1954)
211–12; *Eleven Years of Bible Bibliography,* pp. 499–500.

326. Pedersen, J., *Israel: Its Life and Culture* (2 vols.;
Copenhagen: P. Branner; London: Oxford University Press, 1926, 1940). The Danish original appeared in 1920 (Parts 1–2) and 1934 (Parts 3–4);
some revision was made for the English edition.
This is a permanently valuable contribution to the
study of Israelite life, thought, and institutions. The
poor quality of the English translation makes reading rather difficult.

Cf. JPOS 6 (1926) 222–24; JTS 48 (1947) 72–75.

ANET 327. Pritchard, J. B. (ed.), *Ancient Near Eastern Texts
Relating to the Old Testament* (2nd ed.; Princeton: Princeton University Press, 1955). The purpose
of the work is generally the same as that of Gressmann's volume, though a different selection of texts
has been made and the grouping is according to
literary type. The second edition has some revised
translations and adds some new material. The
work is a real library of ancient Near Eastern
literature which can be used even by nonbiblical
students; though each translator is a specialist, the
student must not accept uncritically any translation.

Cf. JAOS 71 (1951) 259–64; JCS 6 (1952) 124–27; Or

22 (1953) 221–22; JSS 1 (1956) 400–402; Bib 37 (1956) 365–67; JNES 16 (1957) 68–71.

ANEP 328. Pritchard, J. B., *The Ancient Near East in Pictures Relating to the Old Testament* (Princeton: Princeton University Press, 1954). A collection of over 750 pictures arranged according to such subjects as "daily life," "writing," "gods and their emblems," etc. Nearly one hundred pages of text explain the pictures and supply information as to their origin, etc. This work is intended as a companion volume to ANET.

Cf. *Interpretation* 9 (1955) 216–18; ZAW 67 (1955) 129–30; JBL 75 (1956) 77–78; JSS 1 (1956) 186–87; RB 63 (1956) 307–8.

329. Rowley, H. H. (ed.), *The Old Testament and Modern Study* (Oxford: Clarendon Press, 1951). Excellent surveys of the work done between 1920 and 1950 on a variety of biblical topics, e.g., archaeology, Pentateuchal criticism, Psalms, wisdom literature, philology, biblical theology, etc. All contributors are members or honorary members of the Society for Old Testament Study in England.

330. Thomas, D. W. (ed.), *Documents from Old Testament Times* (London: Nelson, 1958). A shorter collection of texts than ANET prepared by members of the Society for Old Testament Study in England; there are brief notes and short bibliographies. A few materials not in ANET have been included. The quality of the translations varies with the authors; generally, ANET is much superior.

Cf. RB 66 (1959) 452–53; *Book List* (1959) 10; JSS 5 (1960) 72–73.

331. Willoughby, H. R. (ed.), *The Study of the Bible Today and Tomorrow* (Chicago: University of Chicago Press, 1947). This is a collection of essays by over twenty scholars who survey in general and special studies work done in both Testaments before World War II and indicate tasks for the future. The work was sponsored by the Chicago section of the Society of Biblical Literature and Exegesis. The papers, naturally, vary in quality, and events in the biblical world have rendered some no longer useful. Still valuable are the articles of Bowman, Rylaarsdam, Orlinsky, and Marcus.

⋆ XXI. Bibliography ⋆

332. Anderson, G. W. (ed.), *Book List* (Printed for Private Circulation). Since 1957 the present editor is responsible for the publication. Copies may be obtained on application to D. R. Ap-Thomas, Llansadrwn, Menai Bridge, Anglesey. Cf. *Eleven Years of Bible Bibliography*. Published annually.

333. Hempel, J. (ed.), "Wichtige Veröffentlichungen in Zeitschriften und Sammelwerken," ZAW. For several years now, each issue of ZAW contains very valuable summaries of important, more or less current articles appearing in journals, series, *Festschriften,* etc., if they have interest for the biblical scholar. These abstracts are prepared by the editor and a few colleagues. The coverage is quite extensive and includes some publications fairly inaccessible to most students. Its counterpart for the NT can be found in "Zeitschriften-Bibliographie" which is published regularly in ZNW.

334. Marouzeau, J. (ed.), *L'Année philologique: Bibliographie critique et analytique de l'antiquité grécolatine* (Paris: Société d'édition "Les Belles Lettres"). It was begun in 1928 with a survey of the years 1924–26, as a supplement to the editor's *Dix années de bibliographie classique 1914–24*. It is an important tool for the NT student, as it covers

several areas in which biblical topics and classical subjects overlap. See the headings such as *Testamenta, Testamentum vetus, Testamentum novum, Archéologie non classique,* etc.

335. Metzger, B. M., *A Bibliography of Bible Study for Theological Students* (Princeton Seminary Pamphlets 1; Princeton: Theological Seminary Library, 1948). "Its aim is to provide a hand list which can be used as a guide to the more important books about the Bible. The list has been restricted to books in the English language except for original texts, dictionaries, and grammars, where the use of foreign languages is indispensable and unavoidable." Data are supplied without comment; very lean on Catholic entries. Second edition, 1960.

336. Metzger, B. M., *Index of Articles on the New Testament and the Early Church Published in Festschriften* (Journal of Biblical Literature Monograph Series 5; Philadelphia: Society of Biblical Literature and Exegesis, 1951). An extremely useful index to articles which are often quite important, but usually overlooked because they have appeared in the limited editions of *mémoires, mélanges, Festschriften,* jubilee volumes, etc. ("the best way to bury a good article"). A supplement to the index appeared in 1955.
Cf. ATR 33 (1951) 261–62; ETL 32 (1956) 87.

336a. Metzger, B. M. (ed.), *Index to Periodical Literature on the Apostle Paul* (New Testament Tools and Studies 1; Leiden: Brill; Grand Rapids, Mich.: Eerdmans, 1960). An excellent, though not exhaustive, bibliography of articles on the thirteen Pauline epistles found in 114 periodicals. The entries are grouped very conveniently under useful subject headings: Bibliographical Articles on Paul, Historical Studies on the Life of Paul, Critical Studies of the Pauline Literature (broken down according to the individual epistles), Pauline Apocrypha, Theological Studies, History of the Interpretation of Paul and of His Work. This is an indispensable tool for the study of the Pauline corpus.

Cf. TS 21 (1960) 643–44.

NTA 337. *New Testament Abstracts. After two experimental issues (Jan. 1956 multilithed; May 1956 printed), the first formal issue appeared in Fall 1956 (Vol. 1, no. 1). Published three times a year by the Jesuits of Weston College, Weston, Mass., it is a record of current periodical literature on the NT. An English survey is made of the NT literature in many languages, including useful summaries of book reviews; it is extremely useful for both the NT specialist and theologians.

338. *Nober, P., "Elenchus bibliographicus," *Biblica*. Since its foundation in 1920, *Biblica* has been publishing bibliographies of books and articles directly and indirectly pertaining to the OT and NT. The present editor issued his first publication in 1949; since that time he has expanded the coverage so that annually the number of entries reaches over 3500. There are no summaries or critiques of books or articles, but there are numerous references to reviews of books. This is an indispensable tool for biblical research.

339. Rowley, H. H. (ed.), *Eleven Years of Bible Bibliography* (Indian Hills, Colo.: Falcon's Wing Press, 1957). A collection of the issues of *Book List* (1946–56) which were prepared for the members of the Society for Old Testament Study in England. It is a very useful descriptive-critical bibliography of a large number of books on the OT and closely related fields. It is being continued by *Book List.*

340. Stier, F. (ed.), *Internationale Zeitschriftenschau für Bibelwissenschaft und Grenzgebiete* (Düsseldorf: Patmos Verlag). A team of contributors abstracts articles on the OT and NT, and in a variety of allied fields. Publication began in 1952 with the first half of the bibliography for 1951–52; Band 6, Heft 1–2 (bibliography for 1958–59) appeared in 1960. The quality of the abstracts is uneven, and coverage is not complete; the work, however, can be a useful supplement to the bibliographies in *Biblica.* Publication is approximately annual.

    Cf. TS 21 (1960) 133–35.

341. Thomsen, P. (ed.), *Die Palästina-Literatur* (Berlin: Akademie Verlag). This monumental work was issued (1908–56) in six volumes, covering the bibliography from 1895–1939; the complete manuscript for a seventh volume, covering 1940–49, awaits printing. After Thomsen's death in 1954, L. Rost and F. Maass supervised the publication of Vol. 6. In 1957–58, Rost and O. Eissfeldt published two parts of a volume (Band A), which had been prepared by Thomsen and cover the years 1878–94;

a third part will conclude this volume. The bibliography embraces the whole range of literature on Palestine, including modern Palestine. Though much of the material will not interest the biblical student, the work remains indispensable for reference.

342. "Bibliographie sémitique," *Orientalia*. The following bibliographies have appeared; the first four were prepared by S. Moscati, and the last two by G. Garbini: 16 (1947) 103–29; 17 (1948) 91–102; 19 (1950) 445–78; 22 (1953) 1*–38*; 26 (1957) 50*–115*; 28 (1959) 59*–90*. These bibliographies cover books and articles. Though the range is wider than the interests of the biblical student, they are very important for the linguistic and philological study of the Bible.

To keep abreast of the books that are appearing or have appeared in the last couple of years, the student may consult the lists of "Books Received" in the various journals; for this purpose, the list in *Biblica* is particularly important.

Most of each issue of TLZ is devoted to survey of theological literature; of this survey, over one third pertains to the Bible. Other journals issue, from time to time, surveys of recent literature, grouped around a single theme; here, TR should be consulted.

For bibliography up to 1950 see the useful list by P. Nober, Bib 32 (1951) xxxiii*–xl*.

★ Index of Modern Authors ★

[References are to the numbered paragraphs unless otherwise indicated.]